The Four Famous Interview Questions

A Guide for Interviewers and Candidates

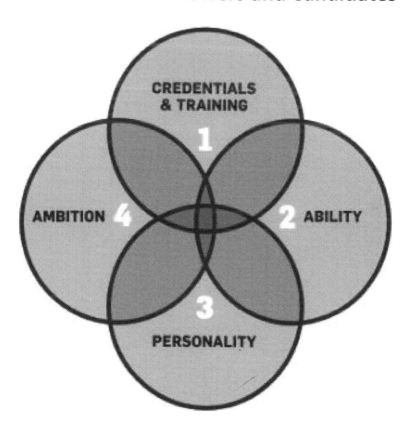

By Bill Ward

Foreword

My first opportunity to be an interviewer came when I was asked to fly to a university campus in San Jose, California to provide technical interviewing support for a job fair our company was involved in. I had no experience or training and—to be honest—hadn't been a very good interviewing candidate in the past. I don't know why I was chosen for the assignment and perhaps several of the first students I interacted with didn't know either.

Sloppy though the experience was, I found that asking interview questions changed the way I thought about responding to them. Because I realized that the whole process is about learning how well the company and the candidate meet one another's needs, I do my best to respond in a way that helps the interviewer understand whether I'll be a good fit for the role they are filling and for their organization.

Now, I have been an interviewer for over 12 years, selecting candidates for a variety of jobs including technicians, engineers, programmers, managers, cooks, dishwashers, operators, and supervisors. I've seen some of the very best and worst kinds of questions asked and I've seen some of the best and worst kinds of responses given.

As my management perspective has matured, I have considered the relationship between what I, as a hiring manager, need to know about the candidate and how I ask the questions. It boils down to how well I can answer for myself the Four Famous Interview Questions about the candidate. In situations where the tables were turned, and I was in the candidate's chair, I realized I needed to answer these four fundamental questions to show I was the person who best fit the need of the hiring organization.

This book is written in the form of an allegory. It is intended that this format will make the information digestible to the reader and illustrate the key points of the interviewing process. Henry Williams originally appeared in my first work entitled Build a Great Career; A Guide for New (and Veteran) Employees. That work focuses on how employees who are new to the business world can avoid costly mistakes and build a solid career by following a set of tips.

I hope you enjoy and find value in this work. I'd love to hear from you via email at Bill@BillWard-Leadership.com

Chapter 1

Henry

Henry Williams jumped up quickly to wipe up the spilled soda on his desk. He'd been jittery all morning as he thought about reviewing candidates with Maria after lunch and had knocked over his glass while reaching for his notepad. He was both excited and nervous about the prospect of selecting an assistant to support him in his role as the Emerging Leaders Coordinator at Powell United.

He had been in the position for three years and had enjoyed a great deal of success. He was promoted after what had become famously known throughout the company as his Mentoring Notebook Project (MNP). Henry had conducted a series of interviews with senior members of the staff at Powell United after he'd learned about gaps in his performance. He learned the value of feedback from people who can provide visibility to one's blind-spots. He created the notebook to capture the advice he received and it became synonymous at Powell with the process of receiving feedback and making changes to improve. Henry's work was summarized into 15 tips to help build a career.[1] Based on his work, all new associates have had the MNP as part of their new employee onboarding and refer to it culturally whenever they

---

[1] Henry's work is chronicled in the book "Build a Great Career" by Bill Ward.

mentioned some feedback or advice they received. Henry had been instrumental in incorporating the principles of the MNP into the performance management system of the company. His role as the coordinator of the Emerging Leaders program at his local facility had gained him a following across the Powell network and his reputation extended into the community including some speeches to the chamber of commerce about the work that Powell was doing.

Henry had been working at the edge of his limit and was eager to have someone to work with him to increase the value of the program. He had worked with Paul, his former supervisor, to craft a job description for the job posting. He'd posted the role internally and externally and 13 candidates had applied. Henry had very little experience in supervision and had only been involved in interviews where he was the candidate. He was nervous about selecting the best candidate. At least he knew enough to realize that the success of his program depended on selecting the right person.

Chapter 2

Henry

This afternoon he was to review the candidates with Maria, his supervisor and the Human Resources manager, to reduce the pool to a manageable number. He hoped to gain some insight into how to choose the best candidates. He had reviewed all candidates and had tried to sort them using a variety of criteria, but he hadn't been able to identify any frontrunners and he couldn't rule anyone out.

He took copies of all the applicant files with him to meet with Maria. As he entered her office, she had soft music playing in the background and it was surprising to Henry how quickly it calmed him. He was anxious about selecting the right candidate but he was almost more worried about seeming incapable in front of someone he respected so much.

Maria rested her hand on Henry's shoulder as she approached and pushed the pause button on her phone that was feeding her Bluetooth speaker system. Standing behind him she looked over his shoulder to see the files in his arms. She furrowed her brow, which Henry didn't see. Returning to her chair she reached across the desk to receive the folders from him. As she quickly reorganized the files in a new order, Henry remembered her extreme organizational penchant. He knew he had much to learn so his attention was rapt.

"Well, let's see how we can arrange these files to better analyze them," Maria said, thoughtfully. Henry pulled out a notepad, realizing he was about to learn a great deal. "Let's first place all internal candidates into one pile, and external candidates in another" she said. After sorting them she asked to see the job description that had been used to create the posting. She read it slowly and attempted to hide her disappointment. In order to help Henry make progress, she knew she had to do some course correction. "Henry, can you please step to the whiteboard to capture some of the elements of the job description? In your view, Henry, what qualifications will be most important to a successful person in this role?"

Henry hadn't even considered this question when creating the job description. He'd simply started with a job description for another role and changed some of the information to describe some of the key responsibilities of this new job. As he considered this, he became very uncomfortable. His face felt hot and he began to sweat. As he stared at his copy of the job description he realized he couldn't find a good answer and he kept his eyes averted from Maria.

She allowed him the pain of the moment, but not for long. "Henry, we've got to back up a few steps to get this right. I own some of the blame for this, but we're not ready to screen these candidates." Maria could sense Henry's shame and she wanted to ease his discomfort since she felt like she'd let him down. "Let me provide you the worksheet that I use when creating a job description and we'll meet on Monday to review what you come up with."

Henry was filled with emotion as he gathered up his files to return to his office. He wasn't sure if he should be more embarrassed or angry and his frustration was visible in his demeanor as he went to his desk, then out the front door to take a long walk around the parking lot.

Alice had provided Henry with a one page worksheet designed to promote a deliberate evaluation of what essential criteria should be used in selecting a candidate. On his way home, Henry determined to study the sheet over a light supper at a local Tapas bar, then think about it while running along the Fish Creek trail. He'd often found that running allowed his mind to review a topic from multiple perspectives. He could process details and, in effect, cross examine his own thoughts while running.

The point of the worksheet was to document the key responsibilities of the role and identify the essential qualifications of a successful employee in that role. It was designed to answer questions in a specific sequence such that one would be directed to a correct overall conclusion. Each section's answers should inform the answer for the subsequent section and should also direct the hiring manager to select the correct candidate by using a need-based process rather than simply selecting a person they enjoyed in the interview.

As Henry finished his supper, he absentmindedly paid his bill, scooped up his gym bag, and went to change into his running clothes. As he drove to the trailhead, he was distracted as he considered what duties he wanted his assistant to be responsible for.

In the parking lot, Henry stretched against the rail fence and tightened up his laces. He had a favorite playlist he liked to run to and as it began to play, he turned the volume all the way up.

After some time, Henry's thoughts drifted from the mechanics of running and his mind returned to the problem of finding a suitable assistant. He considered a list of all the things his role required. He thought about the development of programs, responding to and initiating correspondence with counterparts at other Powell facilities, community outreach activities, and conducting classroom activities with Powell team members.

Henry had to adjust his pace to avoid a turtle that had walked onto the path. The Bluebells were in bloom and he especially enjoyed seeing them in the golden hours of twilight as his mind returned to his problem. Of the duties he currently had on his plate, Henry was thinking about

Figure 1. Andy Stanley speech

which ones truly benefitted from his particular talents compared to the duties that actually distracted him from his areas of strength. He remembered hearing from Andy Stanley that you should only do what only you can do. Of course, Andy was referring to leading an organization from the top but in some small way Henry thought he should consider this principle when creating the job responsibilities for his assistant. Andy Stanley used the example of needing to host events with all the many details that must be arranged. Andy found it to be uninteresting and a distraction from what he's skilled at, but he was able to identify someone who had that passion and found it to be a thrill. This idea of finding the right person for the right kind of work and eliminating the wrong work from certain roles resonated with Henry and he wanted to incorporate it into this activity.

Henry took a quick break to get a drink of water while leaning against a rail overlooking a waterfall. He enjoyed the vista and used the moment to crystalize the thought that was brewing. There were a few things that Henry didn't find satisfying about his job that he felt he could delegate to the right person. His mind went to the logistics of setting appointments, conducting assessment surveys, responding to inquiries about the program, and soliciting guest speakers for the program. These were fundamental needs of the program that he didn't excel at or enjoy. He began to understand, more than ever, the reasoning behind what Andy Stanley was saying and developed some excitement about making changes to the program that could make it even more fulfilling and valuable than it had been until now.

Now that he had a crisp vision of how the addition of an assistant could improve the Emerging Leaders Program, his thoughts migrated back to the other questions prompted by the worksheet Maria had given him. Based on the vision and purpose of the new role, and some of the key responsibilities, he was better able to determine what skills and abilities one must possess as well as what training and experience would most effectively prepare someone for a role such as this. He knew that as he filled out the worksheet he'd have to challenge himself, and potentially defend certain details like education requirements and salary. Being deliberate would help him to create this role properly and get just the right employee. Henry's running pace increased as he returned to his car at the trailhead. He felt a sense of excitement having made such significant progress. As he uploaded the form Maria had given him he created a revision that he hoped she wouldn't mind.

Job Description Worksheet

Powell
United

Job Title:	Department/Hiring Manager:

Purpose and vision of the role:
(What will the position add to the department?)

Key Responsibilities:
(What tasks will this person perform in order to fulfill the purpose and vision of the role?)

Key Skills and Abilities:
(What skills and abilities will this person need to perform their responsibilities?)

Required (or Preferred) Experience, Education and Certifications:
(What experiences and training are required or preferred for this role?—should be able to justify)

Exempt or non exempt employee type:	Consult with HR department for federal guidelines based on role.
Compensation level for this role:	

Job description worksheet, Alice Bergman, Rev 2.3 July 2016

Chapter 4

Henry

Monday at 11:00 sharp Henry returned to Maria's desk with a greater sense of confidence. He provided her the completed worksheet based on his work over the weekend. She reviewed it and saw that he'd added a section she hadn't seen on other versions of the form which he called Purpose and Vision of the role.

"I was reflecting on how I'd define a role that would maximize the value of adding another person to my team," Henry began. He looked past Maria at the calendar on the wall to avoid her eye contact, still feeling the emotions of their previous meeting. "My strengths are in the development and presentation of our program both inside and outside the company. I'm also good at coordinating with the executive team and the Emerging Leader candidates, but where I find the most discomfort is in areas that are more structured and analytical. If I can find someone who can manage logistics and assessments better than I can and who can share in some of the presentation duties, we can really increase the power of what we are doing."

Maria was reminded why they put so much faith in Henry. He had not just learned from the worksheet she had provided, he had taken it to a much higher level than she had seen before. She stood to come around the desk to where Henry was sitting. Looking him right in the eye and placing her right hand on his right forearm she couldn't hide her awe.

"Henry, this is extremely good work. I feel like I let you down by not taking time in advance to help you build an appropriate job profile before you posted it. I'm quite impressed with the way you've defined this role and taken the process to the next level. We'll need to run this by Alice as a recommendation for a new revision of her form but for now, let's use it as you have it." Henry's confidence was restored and he appreciated both the apology and the recognition. He knew, however, that this didn't solve his problem. He still had 13 candidates who applied for a different job than the one he was now trying to fill.

Maria drew him away from his thoughts. "Now that you've created a vision and purpose statement of the role and a list of attributes you want to use as selection criteria, please work with Debbie from my team to convert your worksheet data into the job responsibility template we use. She can help ensure that we are abiding by all legal requirements."

~~~~~~~~~~~~~

Later that day, Paul was surprised to hear again from Henry so soon. "Hey, Buddy, did you fill your position yet? How did that job description work out that we worked on together?" Paul was happy he had provided Henry some help. He missed having Henry on his team and was quite proud of the progress of his former employee.

"Actually, Paul, that's why I'm calling," Henry replied. "You've been so good to me that I wanted to share with you what I learned from Maria about creating job descriptions. Do you have time to get together for lunch tomorrow?"

When they met the next day, Henry hoped that he was sharing the feedback to Paul in a helpful way. It was clear that Paul was interested and open to learning from Henry about the worksheet experience when they had to take an extended lunch to cover all the information. Paul confessed that he felt inadequate as a hiring manager and pled to be included in the additional sessions between Henry and Maria.

Chapter 5

Henry

The following week the group of three agreed to meet over Thai food since they all had very busy schedules and could only find a midday meeting time in common. While the Chicken Satay was being served Henry and Paul listened to Maria very carefully. "Now that we know what the role requires, it's easy to know how to find out which candidates possess the right stuff." The two men nodded thoughtfully and listened intently. "The selection process has at least three phases and I believe the first phase is often overlooked. The resume could be considered the first interview." As Maria looked at the men's expressions, she knew that she'd lost them. They had stopped taking notes and were now focused on the peanut sauce that came with the appetizer. She became a little impatient with them but tried her best to conceal it.

She took a long draw of soda through her straw while she reminded herself that Henry had zero hiring experience and Paul had very little. She took a bite of pork from her plate of drunken noodle while she thought about how best to explain the selection process.

"Guys, let's take a step back," she said, alternating her eye contact slowly back and forth between the two men. "How did you come to select Pad Thai for your lunch, Paul?"

Paul was a little surprised but he began timidly, "I like the fresh taste of the sprouts. I also like the texture of the chopped nuts. I like the way the spicy sauce is absorbed by the noodles and I usually choose chicken because it's a lighter meat and I convince myself that I'm eating healthier than if I chose pork or beef. Unfortunately, I don't care for the texture of tofu."

"Ok," said Maria, cutting him off. "You have a list of criteria including how spicy you like it, the textures, and the healthiness of the dish. You may also have a price target in mind and perhaps there's something familiar about this dish that appeals to you."

Paul and Henry didn't seem to be picking up what she was implying so she slowed down as she continued. "You chose a dish based on how well it met your criteria. You likely have some criteria that are more important than others. For example, I should avoid any dish with pineapple in it because of the acid and there are many that must be cautious because of nut or egg allergies. It's just as likely that there are criteria that are merely matters of preference. On any given day, the criteria might be different for your lunch selection and it's up to you to decide for yourself which choice best meets your needs. You have brought me a job description for Henry's new assistant. It is full of criteria that you have determined to be important to you in selecting the successful candidate. Just as with your lunch choice, the relative importance of individual criteria may vary from essential to preferable. Your job as a hiring manager is to determine which candidate best meets your criteria." Both Paul and Henry seemed to finally get what Maria was trying to say. A few minutes passed by as the three spent some time eating their lunch.

"Now I see, even more, how important the job description is in this process," Henry said, wiping his mouth. "I thought I understood the value when I had my epiphany about what I really wanted from an assistant but now I see that **it must guide the whole hiring process**." He concluded.

"No, It's even more important than that!" Maria interjected further. "The job description even becomes the basis for the expectations that employees are held to and used for evaluations. It's the cornerstone of our selection and performance management strategy. Without it, we have no business employing people at all." She could see in Paul's countenance that he was starting to understand. He absentmindedly crushed some chopped peanut pieces on his plate with his fork while he finished processing this new understanding. When he looked up again to make eye contact with Maria, briefly glancing at Henry, he slowly found words to express the next step that his mind had already leapt to.

"If every job has a job description that is fully developed and accurate, we could even use them when identifying career plans for our team members." He rubbed his forehead with his index finger while he sought for the next phrase. "If someone in my team aspires to a certain role I can use the job description for that role to identify key skills and abilities to help her develop as well as important experiences and certifications to help her prepare for that role." Although he'd started this explanation pensively, he concluded it with confidence.

"Exactly!" Maria said as she signed the credit card statement to pay for their lunch. "We even try to use the job descriptions of key roles to evaluate our bench strength and establish our succession plan. For this reason, we will often recruit people whose qualifications or ambitions exceed those required for the position we currently have open."

Henry had been mostly quiet during the lunch, believing himself to be the most junior member of the team. As they were driving back to work he spoke up. "Maria, thanks for lunch and for educating us on this process. We've learned so much from you today but we didn't make as much progress toward selecting my assistant as I thought we would. I want to propose that I use what we've built so far to review the resumes again to try to reduce the candidate pool. Based on what I've learned from you, I think I can disqualify some of them." The car came to rest at a stoplight and the group waited to take the left turn into their facility. Maria held her tongue for a moment. She felt as though she'd fed them quite a bit and that they needed some time to put the new knowledge into practice but she wanted to protect them from a dangerous mistake.

"Make your initial assessment based on your new criteria using the resumes and candidates you have in hand but please don't discard anything or communicate with any candidates until we've met." While Paul and Henry didn't understand the reasoning yet, they agreed that they'd just sort the candidates into piles to present to Maria. "Guys, one more thing," Maria continued, "I'm pleased to be helping with this process but I must admit I hadn't budgeted my time for it. As a result, I'll need to do some of our meetings outside of office hours so that my other work doesn't suffer." Both men agreed that this was acceptable and as they walked up to the lobby of Powell the two men would get together the following Monday evening at Henry's desk to review the candidates and then set up a later time to bring their results to review with Maria.

Chapter 6

Stacy

Stacy sat at her dining table staring at her phone. She had studied Powell United since she learned of them from a college girlfriend. She had adopted their motto to "Be Good and Do Good" and longed to work at a firm as involved in the communities they serve. She had applied for a position she saw online to be an assistant Emerging Leaders Coordinator at their Springfield office. She had attended a self-development workshop sponsored by the chamber of commerce and had met Henry Williams, who'd come to discuss the value of responding to feedback. She had his business card on the table next to her phone and was building up the courage to call him. It had been three weeks since she'd applied. She was working in a cocktail bar but had already finished her associates degree in Business Administration and was eager to put it to work. She was generally outgoing and vivacious but she was nervous about making this call. Perhaps it was because she wanted this particular job so badly. Finally, she picked up the phone and dialed the number. As the phone rang, she realized she just needed one thing: To know that her application had been received and to know what the next steps would be. Mostly she wanted to emphasize her interest without being a pest.

At the other end of the line she heard Henry's familiar voice, "Powell Springfield, this is Henry. How can I help you?" he said.

"Yes, hello. This is Stacy Koenig and I submitted a resume and applied for your Emerging Leaders Assistant position a few weeks ago, and I just wanted to check on the status of my application." She hoped she hadn't sounded too rushed although she knew that she'd just blurted it out in one breath.

"Ok, yeah, Hey Stacy, how are you?" Henry said as he flipped through the file folder on his desk to find her information. "Yes, I have your paperwork in front of me. To be honest, we had a delay and we're still working through the process of screening candidates. Let me verify I have your correct contact information." He recited her email and phone number, confirming that what he had was accurate. "To be honest, we've revised the job posting and we're comparing the new details against the resumes we have in hand. We should be able to communicate with you by the 12th to let you know if you've made it to the first round of interviews." Stacy was concerned with what she heard. She had carefully crafted her resume for the previous job posting.

"Thank you, I'm very hopeful to join you at Powell. I do have one request, however. I hope this isn't too forward, but would you mind emailing me a copy of the new job posting?" She bit her nails as she waited for his reply. She was concerned that being direct might be off-putting.

Henry wasn't put off in the least by the request and agreed to send her the job posting. They exchanged pleasantries and hung up the phone. Later, as Stacy reviewed the revised document, she became alarmed. On the one hand, the new description was even more in line with her experience and interests. On the other hand, it was clear that her resume did not fit this new job description and she feared she might be disqualified from consideration.

Stacy wasn't sure how to proceed. She discussed it with her friend Jenny at work as they set up for happy hour. "You just need a chance for them to meet you. They'll love you and they'll beg you to take the job," Jenny declared. Jenny was a good friend and a great listener. For this reason, she earned a lot in tips from the bar's regular patrons. Unfortunately for Stacy, Jenny's ambition was limited to getting the premium shifts where they worked.

"I think I'll do well *if* I can meet them but I'm pretty sure that my resume won't open the door." She explained to Jenny.

"Then just send them a new resume." Jenny offered as she popped her gum, flipped her ponytail and scampered off to welcome a group of frat-boys to their table. Stacy struggled with this idea. It wasn't the first time she thought about it, but it was the first time she considered doing it. She contemplated the idea throughout the evening and finally determined to do it. If she was bold enough to call, then to request a new job description, she could safely send a new resume. In the end, she realized that the risk was low. If she didn't provide a new resume, she could be disqualified. If she offended Henry through her forwardness, the cost would be no higher.

Chapter 7

Stacy

Stacy had developed a good relationship with one of the professors in her degree program and asked to meet her over breakfast at a local coffee shop. She provided a copy of the original job description and her first resume as well as the new job description and the beginnings of her new resume. "Joan, thanks for taking time to help me recraft my resume this morning," Stacy said as they watched the handsome barista preparing their drinks. "Getting this job would mean the world to me and I feel like I need a little help based on the circumstances."

"Of course," Joan responded, as she took one more glimpse of the large biceps of the barista. "I'm happy I can be there for you. I hope it's helpful."

Joan had enjoyed getting to know her student during the last two years. When she was new to the community, Stacy had given her lots of tips about the best shops in town and had introduced her to her chiropractor, who did miracles for her. Joan had been a corporate recruiter for several years prior to returning to academia, believing this would be a greater opportunity to provide meaningful help to the rising generation of leaders. She'd seen great promise in Stacy and was eager to assist her in any way she could.

Stacy and Joan looked together at the new job description. Joan agreed that this job seemed like a great fit for Stacy. "Let's review what questions this job posting is asking," Joan said as they got down to business. "The employer has about three opportunities to find out if you are the right person for this job. In this economic climate, companies are working as lean as possible. If you can only have a few employees in your team, it's even more important that you make the right choice. The struggle for the employer is difficult. They must make a decision that can have a huge impact based on a few snapshots about the candidate. Therefore, every aspect of the recruiting and hiring process must be very efficient and deliberate." Joan looked Stacy in the eye and attempted to assess her understanding of what she had just explained. Satisfied that Stacy was on the same page, she continued with a question. "What does Powell want to know about all the applicants to this job?"

Stacy stared at the job description for a moment. She read aloud the job summary:

"Powell United is expanding its Emerging Leaders Program to better serve the development of its employees. We are seeking someone who is enthusiastic, customer-service-oriented and who possesses a passion for helping others. Essential responsibilities include (1) event planning and hosting of training sessions, (2) developing relationships with external organizations in order to solicit and arrange guest lecturers, and (3) conducting assessments of training effectiveness. Some expertise in course development and delivery is also a plus."

As she did so, she thought about her experience and how she could rephrase her resume. She looked at Joan with a look that betrayed her confusion. She was stumped and couldn't conceal it from her friend.

"Think of it like this," Joan offered. "There are four key questions that every hiring manager needs to answer to know if you are a good candidate for the role." Stacy reached for her note pad, expecting Joan to provide a full download of her thinking. Joan had a different approach in mind.

"The first key question is whether you have the necessary education, training, certifications, or licensure for the role in question. For many occupations, there are regulatory requirements that must be met in order to employ a person." As examples Joan referenced Pharmacists, Lawyers, Accountants, and Pilots. "This first question about a person represents a Go/No-Go criterion. If the role requires a specific training or certification, no candidate without them can be considered." Joan's eyes then brightened up and stated that the listed education and training may not be a strict requirement but a preference. It can sometimes be deduced from the job posting, but not always. "Employers tend to advertise the requirements of the ideal candidates but there are some employers who will accept a certain amount of career experience in lieu of education and training in cases where there are not strict certification requirements."

Over the weekend, Henry had been reviewing the resumes he had received to compare them with the job description they had worked on. He noticed that most of the resumes didn't align well with the job description. He wondered how this happened and how he would ever select a suitable candidate. As he sat on his balcony drinking sweet tea, he felt dejected, like he was failing in his first hiring attempt. As he watched the Sunday sunset, he had a thought. He grabbed the original job description that he and Paul had created and found that some of the resumes matched this version quite well. As he contemplated the situation he was in, he realized that the mistake they'd made would delay their selection process.

Monday morning Henry sent Paul an email explaining his findings and recommended that when they met later in the day they'd decide how to make it right. Henry was still very sensitive about his reputation and didn't like to call attention to failures or weaknesses. Paul didn't have the same sense of self preservation and was willing to admit mistakes more readily. He recommended in his email reply that perhaps they should send a note to each candidate explaining that there had been a change and that the job description had been revised. "We can just request a revised resume from each of them and put a deadline of Friday. If we don't get any viable candidates from this group we can repost the job and start from scratch," Paul reasoned. Henry didn't disagree so he crafted the email over his lunch and send it out to each candidate. He postponed the meeting with Paul until after they had the revised resumes but decided they should still meet with Maria to see what more they could learn from her about their process.

Maria could meet them on Wednesday evening but only for about 30 minutes. They determined to meet in her office and Henry brought an oversized bar of Toblerone chocolate to share as they spoke. "There are several questions we must answer about each candidate," Maria explained. "I tend to refer to them in a certain sequence because if a candidate fails to pass any of the questions, there's no reason to move on to the others. The resume is usually most useful for getting a glimpse into answering the first question; which is whether the candidate has the required education, training, certifications and experience to perform the role."

"Henry, what education requirement did you put on your posting?" Henry responded that he had placed a requirement for a Bachelor of Business Administration (BBA) degree on the requirements list. "Why that degree?" Maria asked.

Henry stammered for a moment while he tried to recollect what his logic had been for establishing that requirement. "Well," he began, "I have a BBA and it was a requirement for the job I applied for at Powell. In fact, many of the people in our departments have a business background." Maria observed his discomfort briefly as his disposition changed. He began to recognize he didn't have Maria's support for such a requirement. In fact, she appeared to be on the attack.

"Which of the classes from your curriculum do you rely on most in this role? Tell me, is it Accounting or Economics?" Henry had never seen Maria like this. He held his tongue and allowed her to continue. "Maybe it was Finance or Statistical Analysis," she blurted out. She took another triangle of the chocolate treat and allowed it to melt in her mouth as she took several deep breaths. She offered no apology but was much more calm when she resumed. "I handed you the worksheet to use in building a job description for this purpose. What are the courses from your degree program that are of greatest use in the role you are in?"

Henry was still feeling timid but he explained to her that there were a few key courses that had helped him including Business Strategy, Business Communication, and Behavioral Theory. "In fact, if there was a degree program that included just these courses I'd accept that." Henry was a bit bashful at this point and Maria wasn't letting him off the hook yet.

"There are some great degrees that are actually tailored for a role like this one. I'm sorry I've been so aggressive just now but I think its lazy to just call out a degree requirement simply because many of the people in the company have that degree. In fact, if we get too many people with the same perspective and training we run the risk of overlooking other relevant points of view."

Henry looked at Paul briefly and they shared a grim expression, as if to say *Strike two*.

"I think we'd better call it an evening," Maria said. As they gathered their files and pens there was no eye contact and no words were spoken. As the two men excused themselves through her office door, Maria called behind them. "I want to be sure you two are taking this seriously. Otherwise, you are wasting your time and mine. If you aren't going to do the work, I'll simply select someone to fill your vacancy and you can just deal with what you get."

Chapter 9

Stacy

Stacy's heels made a familiar click, click, click as she came up the hallway toward Joan's office. She was right on time and had a picnic-style lunch stored in her backpack as an expression of gratitude for Joan's generous offer to spend time with her improving her resume.

"There are several resume types," Joan began. "And there are many opinions about which is the right version for which kind of candidate and for what type of company the job is in. Four types are commonly referred to: **1) chronological, 2) functional, 3) combination, or 4) targeted."**

Stacy had brought notes from a job search workshop she'd attended and as she set her yogurt container aside she turned to the material she'd received about resume building. "It says here," she said, looking up to see Joan grab a handful of cashews, "that the chronological resume is the most popular and considered to be the traditional format. Its best for those who have a continuous job history and can use their previous job roles to demonstrate accumulation of the required skills for the new job requirements." Stacy reached into her backpack to grab an example of the chronological resume format to refresh herself on its look.

Joan interjected that the strength of the chronological resume is to demonstrate career longevity and a history of increasing responsibility. "What the chronological does not offer, however is an easy way to summarize what you consider to be your strengths." Joan took a drink of water and continued. "Many recruiters and hiring managers are looking for keywords in your resume, even to the extent of using computer software to screen resumes for them." She could see that Stacy didn't quite follow what she meant so she continued. "Let's assume that a company has determined that a key requirement of a certain job is to have experience with the Success-Factors Human Capital Management Software Suite as an administrator. They can efficiently use a program to search thousands of resumes to find people with that specific experience." Stacy began nodding her head slowly, able to process the information Joan had just provided. Joan continued, "While the chronological resume prioritizes experience, the functional resume allows you to focus on your skills and abilities with added search functionality. Some people believe that the functional overly deprioritizes a person's career experience so a third type of resume has emerged called a combination or hybrid resume."

The two ladies each took a few bites of their sandwiches as they thought. "It sounds like a combination resume is what I should write, then," Stacy stated, sounding more like a question.

Joan hesitated for a moment, still relishing the taste of her sandwich. "Let's not rule out the targeted resume." Joan began as she reached across her desk to some papers she'd laid out for this meeting. "We only have a few minutes before I have to excuse myself for a department meeting but let's look at this. A targeted resume is a very useful tool when you can tie your experience and training to the specific requirements of a job. In this case, you have just one job that you are shooting for and it makes sense to customize your resume. The downfall is that it's very time-consuming and it can be difficult to manage a whole library of different resumes for someone in broad job search mode." Joan stood to excuse herself. "Thanks so much for lunch today, it was delicious. Here is an example of how you might create a targeted resume for a specific job posting. Please consider this approach and when you've decided what to do, please email me a copy of your resume as you complete it. We can review it together over the phone in a few days. I should go now but it's been quite nice spending time with you today."

Stacy reviewed the paperwork that Joan had given her. It was a good example that seemed easy to understand. [2]

Sample Help Wanted Ad for Human Resources Manager

Recruit all exempt and non-exempt employees. Orient new employees to the organization. Design and implement staff training and development programs. Manage employee retention initiatives.

Administer all compensation, benefit, and government mandated programs including processing of enrollments, terminations, unemployment, and worker's compensation claims. Responsible for compliance with state and federal labor laws. Serve as COBRA administrator for the company. Member of union contract negotiating and management team.

Human Resources Manager Targeted Resume Sample

Summary of Qualifications

- Experienced manager with expertise in human relations and project management
- Extensive background in staff recruitment and retention
- Staff training and development
- Superb written and oral communication skills
- Organizational and Strategic Planning
- Management Coaching
- Program Marketing
- Contract negotiation and compliance

---

[2] https://www.thebalance.com/how-to-write-a-targeted-resume-2063193

- Knowledge of Federal and State Employment Law

Work History
Benefits Manager, First Bank of the Woods, Denver CO
5/2012-present
- Managed transition from existing health coverage to comply with the ACA (Affordable Care Act)
- Negotiated 1% reduction in premiums by revising benefit package options.
- COBRA coordinator

HR Generalist, Kofax Sporting Goods, Biloxi, MI
6/2008-4/2012
- Processed all hiring and promotion activities
- Processed all separations and conducted exit interviews
- Developed and led all new employee orientation onboarding activities.

Recruiter, Jets Air Transport, Buffalo, NY
12/2006-5/2008
- Conducted all recruiting and hiring activities for 45 ppl/year
- Processed terminations for 12 ppl/year
- Planned and executed employee appreciation events

Education: Bachelor's in Human Resources, Colorado State University, graduated 6/2006

As Stacy considered it, she realized that a targeted resume was probably going to be her best approach. She rushed off to her shift at the bar, but throughout the evening couldn't stop thinking about which skills she had that directly translated to the job posting she'd received from Powell United. At her break, she pulled out the job posting she'd brought from home and doodled her responses on it.

Powell United

Emerging Leaders Program Assistant Coordinator

Powell United is expanding its Emerging Leaders Program to better serve the development of its employees. We are seeking someone who is enthusiastic, customer service oriented and who possesses a passion for helping others

Key Responsibilities

Essential responsibilities include (1) event planning and hosting of training sessions, (2) developing relationships with external organizations in order to solicit and arrange guest lecturers, and (3) conducting assessments of training effectiveness. Some expertise in course development and delivery is also a plus. Other responsibilities may arise, as required, from time to time.

Key Skills, Abilities and Experience

Required:

- Proficiency in MS Excel, PowerPoint, Project and Outlook
- Excellent written and spoken communication skills
- Passion for customer service
- 5 Years' experience in managing and hosting events and bookings
- Customer Service experience
- Professional appearance and demeanor

Preferred:

- Experience developing and delivering classroom instruction materials
- Experience with development and analysis of customer feedback surveys
- Experience in an employee development role

Education Required:

Bachelors of Business Administration

She realized that she met almost all of the requirements. She was excellent with people and had a passion for helping them. Her mother had tried to instill in her the ability to anticipate people's wishes and needs. This became a very handy set of traits in the hospitality industry. Her managers had always relayed positive feedback from customers to her and her tips were generous. Almost as important, to her, was that she was often requested by repeat customers for special events. She knew that if she could capture it properly, she could leverage these skills in this new role. She thought about how best to reflect the portability of these skills..

After her shift, she declined the invitation from the bartender to hang around for a little while. She was eager to get home and finish her resume. She grabbed an order of wings from the kitchen on her way out and rushed to her apartment. It had a beautiful view overlooking the neon lights of several local clubs and the foot traffic gathered around the lighted fountain the city had put in the previous fall.

She set out to build her resume, targeted to this job description. She laid the job description and a blank paper side by side on her desk. Determined to follow the advice Joan had given, she translated her experience into language matching the "questions" asked by the job description. She spent about an hour on this new version of her resume and felt good about the final product. She closed her blinds and retired to bed. As she dozed off her mind reflected on the words she had chosen to demonstrate her eligibility.

Stacy Koenig

Asst. Emerging Leaders Coordinator

Stacy@koenigfamily.net   (123) 555 1234   835 Carolina Avenue

I wish to expand my opportunities by leveraging my interpersonal and organizational skills to help strengthen aspiring leaders.

Professional Expertise

- Event Planning
- Customer Service
- MS Office Suite
- Strong Communication skills
- Project Management
- Networking

Education and certification

Microsoft Office Specialist (MOS) Master certification
A.S. in Business Administration, Leadership specialization

Experience

Waitress/Special Events Coordinator, Louigi's Fountain View   4/2014-Present
- Accept convention bookings and oversee catering and logistics
- Coordinate with florists, bakeries and musicians to ensure guest satisfaction
- Provide excellent customer service to daily customers and event guests

Wedding Coordinator, Hashplains Event Center   2/2012-4/2014
- Plan, schedule and oversee weddings
- Serve as central point of contact and liaison for guests and vendors
- Increased wedding bookings by 14% year over year through sales efforts
- Developed and hosted annual 'bridal bash' to showcase local vendors

Food Server/Catering Captain, The Blue Shark   1/2010-2/2012
- Ensure a pleasant dining experience for all guests
- Coordinate kitchen and wait staff at catering events

Chapter 10

Henry

Paul and Henry, still embarrassed by their last meeting with Maria, determined that they should get together to review the resumes over the weekend. They had suffered a few embarrassing meetings and knew they needed to step up their game. Henry, becoming more assertive as they went through this process together, began by explaining to Paul what Maria had said about what she called her four famous questions.

"The questions," Henry began, "are listed in sequence. Each one can be thought of as a gate. If you don't pass any one of the questions, the others don't matter." He pulled a graphic out of his bag that Maria had given him.

The Four Famous Questions of Interviewing

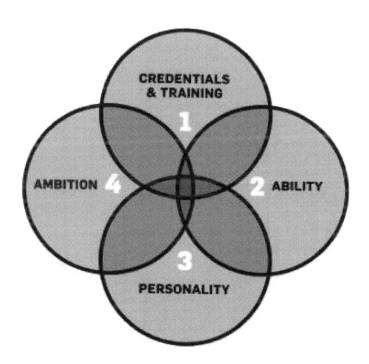

"Let's first scan through the resumes and filter for the credentials and training that folks have. If they don't have the proper training, it doesn't matter how well their other qualities match what we are looking for."

"Sure," Paul said. "I think I understand that. If they don't have any required credentials or training, they are simply disqualified. But, I remember how mad Maria got when she learned about the education requirement we put onto the job description. Do you really want to stick to that degree as a requirement?" Paul asked with sincerity although he worried that Henry might take it as sarcasm based on their previous interaction on the topic. Luckily, Henry didn't take it that way since he'd already been thinking about this issue and had come up with a solution.

"No," Henry said quickly. "I don't want to worry about whether they have a specific degree as much as I want to verify they have some evidence of proficiency, both in the required software and in event management. Let's make that our first criteria to use as a filter."

In the weeks since they first posted the job, the 13 original resumes had grown to 16, even having filtered out a few already.

They sat in near silence as they each took half the pile of resumes and put each in either a yes pile or a no pile based on whether they had software and event management listed on their resume. After reviewing a few resumes they recognized that there were some candidates who had one requirement or the other so it was less clear cut. Also, some people claimed to be good at PowerPoint and Word but not Excel or Outlook. They decided to create three piles of resumes which they named: Yes (all requirements are met), Maybe (some requirements are met) and No (no requirements are met). Maria had explained the meanings of the other three famous questions but it wasn't clear how to know from the resume whether someone was a good fit or had the ability to learn the specific role. For now, they were willing to let their three piles be a sufficient effort as they prepared to present their work to Maria. They had narrowed the candidate pool from 16 total to seven in the yes pile, three in the no pile, and six in the maybe pile. It did feel like they were making progress, but they had only reduced the pile from 16 to 13.

Chapter 11

Henry

Maria appeared tired as they gathered at the coffee shop to review the results of the resume screening. "Let's see what you have," Maria said as she pushed some loose hair out of her eyes and up behind her ear. "You took in additional resumes so you started the screening process with 16 candidates. How many did you disqualify?"

The two men looked at each other and down at the table. "Um, we disqualified three," Henry finally uttered. "They didn't have any of the software experience we require and they didn't have any experience managing or hosting events."

Maria studied the men carefully. "Do you know what question the resume is supposed to help answer?" She asked.

"Yes," Paul responded. "We should be able to determine if they have the required skills for the job based on training, education or experience."

"Do the remaining 13 candidates possess the key skills and abilities your job requires?" she asked. Again, looking at the two men, back and forth, almost burning their eyes with her gaze. She was surprised that these two star employees were having such a difficult time grasping the concepts she was trying to teach them. She'd had a difficult day and had many things to do that evening and wished this meeting had started off better. "About half of the remaining candidates have everything we're looking for and the other half only possess some of what we need." Henry said. He was eager to explain to Maria that they had taken this responsibility seriously and that they didn't intend to fail her.

"We looked at each resume and used the two criteria to filter them. They needed to have event management experience and they needed to be skilled on several specific Microsoft software programs." Henry continued, "We put three into the no pile since they didn't have either. We put another six into the maybe pile because they either had only some of the software we required or they were missing the event management experience." He smiled as he saw Maria's face manifest some relief. "There are seven who claim to have all the skills we highlighted as essential."

"That is a big relief," Maria said. "I understand the desire to not discard candidates that could maybe do the job, even if they only lack some of the skills you are seeking. However, if you have several candidates that possess all the skills you need it doesn't make any sense to entertain candidates who you already know lack skills that you'd have to consistently mentor for or make up the difference for. After all, you are hiring someone to make your job easier, not harder." She slowly glanced at each of the nine disqualified resumes and confirmed their findings as she did. "Please hand these to our Human Resources business partner to have her send out our typical rejection notifications. Now, let's focus on how to decide which of these seven remaining candidates you are going to select." She added more sugar to her cooling coffee and stirred as she finished reviewing the remaining resumes in the pile and slowly removed one more from the pile and set it in the rejection pile. Henry glanced at it atop the pile and recognized it as one he'd agonized over. The person's event planning had been all informal parties he'd thrown as a member of his college fraternity. Henry agreed that this wasn't quite what he was looking for. Maria brushed the crumbs from the table onto her plate as she prepared to leave the meeting. She asked the two men to create several questions they could use for the next step of the process, the phone screen. She reminded them that they should focus a couple questions each on how they would verify the candidates did indeed have the skills they claimed to have as well as how they might understand answers to the other three famous questions. She reminded them that this process had gone on quite a while already and that they should do their best to be ready for phone screens on the final six candidates in the next few days. She recommended a Thursday evening meeting at Henry's desk. Paul offered to bring some bagels and cream cheese but Maria recommended sweets instead. With that, she was gone. Paul and Henry agreed to spend time together over lunch on Tuesday working on their next questions.

Chapter 12

Stacy

Joan carefully unfolded Stacy's resume and the job posting as they sat down at the sandwich shop. They had both ordered the Noah's Half an Arc meal which was a delightful small sandwich with a variety of meats and cheese served with kettle fried potato chips and a soft drink.

"Let's think about how to prep for your phone screen in terms of the Four Famous Interview Questions," Joan began. "You've done a good job here. This is a very nice approach to the targeted resume. I can clearly draw the lines between what experiences you have and what they are looking for. It is simple and clear without a lot of visual noise." Stacy was pleased to hear that she'd done a good job.

Joan continued, "To review, interview questions are all geared to verify that you 1) have the proper training and required certifications to do the work and that you 2) have or can develop the ability to perform the work." Stacy was nodding her head as she listened to Joan. She'd heard about the Four Famous Interview Questions before but was eager to capture new insights as she prepared for the scheduled phone interview. "Once an employer is confident that you can do the job, they'll want to be sure that 3) you will be a good fit for their organization. These often includes questions about your work ethic or your approach to problem solving. Finally, employers want to know 4) what your level of ambition is. This usually refers to your career aspirations." Stacy, finished copying down the last details in her notes as Joan stood to refill her lemonade.

Joan returned to the table, pushing her brown hair back into an elastic band to get it off her face. She sat and took a sip of her drink. As she turned her gaze to Stacy, she resumed. "You won't hear the interviewer ask if you can do the job. If it were that easy, the interview process would be much simpler and quicker. The trick is to translate the question that is asked into one of the four famous questions." She wiped her lips with her napkin as she evaluated Stacy's response to assess her understanding.

"I'll show you how I prepare for an interview." Joan said as she reached across the table for the job posting and a blank sheet of paper. "I usually keep a notebook with me when I'm in job search mode and I capture two to three pages of notes for each role. I also have that notebook in front of me to capture notes during the phone screen and in the face-to-face interview. As I capture notes in the notebook, I also refer to it to keep my mind on the specific examples of experience I want to leverage in the interview."

Stacy watched intently as Joan began the notes by putting the name of the role across the top of a fresh piece of paper. "Let's fill this out together to help you prep for the phone interview. As we go through the job responsibilities, we will want to think about what questions we need to answer and what experience you have that will demonstrate you are prepared for and able to perform this role. I'll captured a few headers from a review of the job responsibilities that are listed," Joan said. Stacy and Joan identified "classroom instruction", "software experience", "event planning" and "customer service". Joan looked up from writing their notes and said, "Let's spend some time capturing the examples you'll want to reference for each of these topics."

"You don't need to write essays on these topics, this is just a series of prompts to assist in your prep. I usually use this exercise to serve as a brainstorming session. I HATE to be stuck in the interview, stalling while thinking about an example that will answer the questions. If I have to think of an example on the spot I may end up with one that doesn't best showcase my talent. I've even accidentally chosen examples that made me look stupid. It's best to be prepared with the right examples of your best work. Since its easy to be nervous in the interview, I also use this prep sheet to capture things I'll want to review several times, especially just before I go into the interview so it will be fresh in my mind."

After working together for an hour, they captured some solid examples of how Stacy's experiences make her a great choice for the position. She could see that the notes would be a valuable way to prep for the interview and was grateful for Joan's guidance and the time they spent together working on it.

Emerging Leaders Program Assistant Coordinator—Powell United
Helping Others

Customer Service Passion
Go extra mile for guests who want special ordered drinks. Get many repeat customers from catering jobs—elizabeth broadhurst example.

Event Planning and Hosting
Governor's daughter's big wedding
State senate's new year's party

Software expertise
Microsoft Office Specialist (MOS) Master certification
Tutored students in word and excel
Created and shared excel macros to simplify bar inventory
Used vlookup and hlookup to organize catering clients for marketing
Used mail merge function to send marketing materials

Classroom Presentation
Toastmaster experience
TLI seminar on icebreaker ideas

Education Relevance
Posting calls for bachelor although I have associates.
Classes I have completed include lower division accounting and finance, Business Strategy, Business Communication and Behavioral Theory.

Chapter 13

Henry

Paul and Henry spoke as they walked through the parking lot to Henry's townhome. Paul carried two six packs of craft beer from the Tin Cannon Brewing Company that had recently become available at their favorite local pizza joint, and Henry carried a large Neapolitan Pizza for the two to share while they created their list of questions. Upon setting themselves up at the dining table inside Paul volunteered to act as scribe while they discussed the four questions.

"To screen the resumes, we used two specific requirements to satisfy question 1, "do you have the required education, training or certification?" We said they needed to have event management experience and they needed to be skilled on several specific Microsoft software programs," He said. "What questions should we ask to understand their abilities? I know we need to ask open-ended questions to give them an ability to explain themselves."

Henry broke in with a couple of questions about specific tasks in MS Office that would help them to assess actual ability. Paul wrote down the questions and listened while Henry continued. "We should ask the candidates to explain an example of a more advanced project they completed integrating different Office tools. Also, we will need the candidate to use the mail merge function. That's tricky enough that it would be great to have someone who already knows that," Henry said while Paul nodded and continued to write.

"If we can verify these things about their Office skills we should move on to their event planning skills," Paul said. "I haven't done much event planning myself so I'm not sure how to evaluate that."

"It's much more difficult than you would expect," Henry interjected. "We're not throwing weddings and proms but there are a lot of details that aren't obvious if you haven't done it. I'll just ask them to describe a typical event that they've managed. If that doesn't give us a lot of satisfaction, I can follow up with explaining an event that would be typical for the candidate to have to plan and host and see what they believe the steps should be."

Paul wrote down a synopsis of what Henry had just said and laid his pen down while he opened another beer. "One last thing we should get out of the phone screen and that's a sense of their personality and how they go about their work," he said.

Henry said thoughtfully, "I'd like to ask each of them the same question so that it will be a fair comparison between the candidates. I'm thinking about a question that reveals how they manage conflicting priorities in an environment where there is more to do than time allows." Paul nodded his head in acknowledgment. He's heard this type of question asked often in interviews and it was worded almost just as Henry had stated it.

The pizza was gone, the beer half-gone, and both men were starting to get weary. The men decided they had what they needed for the phone screens and agreed to be done for the evening. Henry argued with Paul for a few moments, finally prevailing in getting him to take the leftover beer home with him.

Chapter 14

Henry

Gathered together in a small conference room, Maria, Henry, and Paul sat around the conference phone. They each had a pad of paper, a stack of resumes, and a drink. They had blocked out the afternoon to conduct phone screens and review their candidates. Company policy was to bring the top three candidates on site for an in-person interview which they hoped to complete two weeks hence. Maria had agreed to sit in on the interviews and to try to allow the two men to conduct the interview. She had reviewed the questions which had been crafted and gave them additional questions to add to their list.

They had agreed on a format. Each man was to have ownership of specific questions. They would also own the follow up questions to clarify the answer and get the right level of detail. They'd convert the answers to their questions into a numeric value and keep them in a spreadsheet so that they'd be able to objectively evaluate the candidates' interview performance. Finally, they agreed on a visual signal that any of the three could give to indicate that the interview should be concluded without going on.

Lewis Hall had been informed by a corporate recruiter that he should expect a phone call this afternoon. Henry and Paul were nervous as they dialed his number but Maria's presence calmed them somewhat.

After dialing the number, the three waited through four rings until they heard the candidate pick up the phone, "Hello?" said the voice on the other end of the call.

"Yes, Hello, this is Henry Williams from Powell United. Is this Mr. Hall?"

After some indistinguishable sounds on the other end, they heard a reply. "Yes, this is Lewis Hall. Hello, how are you?" Giving the others a quizzical look, Henry replied. "Hello Lewis, this is Henry Williams and I'm here with Paul and Maria from Powell United. Is this still a good time to chat with you about your application to our Emerging Leaders Program Assistant Coordinator position?"

After another moment and more strange noises, Lewis replied. "Uh, yeah, I'm available for a few minutes." Maria held up her hand in jest giving the end of the interview sign, and gently laughed as she shook her head.

"Ok, Lewis," Henry forged onward, "Let's start by letting you tell us a bit about your background and why you are interested in this role."

"Sure," Lewis said. "I have been working as an office manager at the university for the last three years after completing my bachelor's degree in business administration. I am responsible for ensuring that the office has all the necessary office supplies and I am the face of the department to all visitors to the office. This includes students, parents, faculty, and staff. I even represent the department to the administration from time to time as well as to the public." Maria gave the other two men a look and a nod that seemed to say "he's pulled it together" and they responded with a similar nod while Lewis continued. "I supervise student employees and assist them in their duties. I often find myself mentoring them in MS Office skills. I guess what interests me about this position is that I'll be able to assist in the development of leaders in your company. It feels like the next step from what I've been doing but taking it from academics to private industry."

"Thank you," Paul said as Lewis finished. "I see from your resume that the office you manage reports to the accounting department."

Before Paul could finish his thought, Lewis interrupted. "Yes, we report to the accounting department but we also have responsibility to support any overflow needs of the college of business plus an occasional request from the office of the president." Paul had wanted to ask about his customer service skills but thought that maybe he'd just learned about

Lewis' ability to listen patiently and answer the correct question. He didn't want to assume the worst of Lewis but now he had at least one data point and determined to watch for a trend of this behavior.

"Thanks, Lewis. I wanted to ask you to tell us about a time where you were asked to perform a duty that extended beyond your normal responsibilities and how you handled it," Paul was finally able to get the question out.

He looked at Maria and Henry but didn't recognize any dismay on their faces. He decided that, perhaps, he'd judged too harshly.

"Yes, sometimes that happens. I realize that I have an opportunity to add value in lots of ways and I go out of my way to do what I can to help."

Paul broke back in, interrupting Lewis. "Can you tell us about a specific experience that showcases your approach?"

Suddenly there was a moment of silence on the other end of the line. It was almost 20 seconds before they heard Lewis begin again. "Sure, I'll tell you about the time we held our Founder's Day celebration and the Mayor had changed his mind about attending with very short notice. We had several activities planned for Friday evening and for all day Saturday. As late as Wednesday, the Mayor said he and his office team couldn't attend because of a conflicting engagement. We'd picked up all the supplies for the participant packets Thursday midday and had spent several hours putting the packets together. Several students had volunteered to work on the packets and we bought pizza to feed them." Paul looked at Henry and Maria and wondered if he should break in. He had already interrupted him once so he decided to be patient to see where this was going.

"After all the packets were assembled and the supplies were exhausted, we cleaned up the office and sent everyone home. I was just about to shut out the lights and lock the doors when the phone rang. It was the secretary to the mayor calling to let us know that their conflict had fallen through so they'd be happy to attend our celebration."

"Anyway, to make a fairly long story a little shorter, I had to find out how to get another dozen packets made up, which included going to several suppliers to get all the items included in the packets. I was lucky to get it all together in time so that the folks from City Hall could enjoy our event. Later, the College President learned of my effort and awarded me a token of his appreciation at a meeting of the senior faculty." Lewis wrapped up his explanation, reliving the pride of that achievement.

Paul asked a follow up question. "Why did you have to do all of that work by yourself?"

Lewis responded fairly quickly, "Normally, I do rely heavily on delegation because I think it's a good way to develop people and spread the work. In this case, however, I already had the relationships with all the suppliers, and a car, and I thought it was too important to risk failure so I decided to get it done quickly myself."

"Thank you, Lewis," Henry began, "this is Henry. How much of the Founder's Day event were you in charge of planning?"

"For this event, I was only responsible for the participant packets. I have, however, been responsible for smaller full events in the past. Would you like me to tell you about one of those events?" Paul bristled a little, thinking this was another example of Lewis not listening carefully but Henry didn't seem to be offended.

"Sure, that would be fine," Henry replied.

"At the beginning of each spring semester we hold an event where graduate students present selected papers to local business leaders. It's become a bit of a tradition and I've been honored to be the planner and host of the event for the last two years."

"Good," Henry said, "let's talk about that one. Please describe your level of involvement and tell us about a mishap and how you recovered from it."

Lewis cleared his throat. "What normally happens is that the Accounting Dean tells me the theme of the conference and I'm given the authority to make all required arrangements. I clear several specific details with the Dean, such as who I'll invite from the business community to attend. I also have the honor of inviting someone to give a key note speech and I verify that the Dean is ok with my choice." Lewis paused to allow for questions but hearing none, he continued. "Aside from that I book the room, register the students who will be presenting, arrange for all the audio equipment and coordinate with hospitality to provide the continental breakfast, beverage service, and a buffet lunch." Lewis stopped speaking, believing that there was nothing more to say on the topic. Henry and Paul gave each other a look of satisfaction with what they heard.

Maria spun her finger in the air toward the men to indicate, "let's keep it moving." Paul complied by asking the next question. "Ok, Lewis. This is Paul again. As you know from the job posting, we need someone who has proficiency in MS Office applications. Can you tell us how the mail merge function works?"

Lewis responded to this question and several other questions about Microsoft functions. At length, the interview ended and Henry and Paul thanked Lewis for his time and advised him that he'd hear from the HR department within seven business days.

Chapter 15

Stacy

Joan and Stacy giggled as they gave each other a simultaneous eye roll at the flirty cashier's attempt at over-supplying Chick-Fil-A sauce as some sort of demonstration of benevolent power. They chose a corner seat, near the window and away from the children's playground. "I'm glad you were able to put together your prep sheet for tomorrow's interview," Joan started to get the conversation going. "What I'd like to do is go over a few potential questions for the interview and I can give you feedback to help improve your responses. Mock Interviews can prove to be a very powerful way to prepare for real interviews for a few reasons. They can help point out potential questions that you might not have thought of and they can give you a chance to practice your responses so that when the real interview comes you have a polished answer. I often find that having practice with interview questions, I'm less nervous in the real interview and more confident. One final benefit comes from the feedback you can get. This feedback can be very valuable in getting good at interviewing."

"Joan, I'm thankful for your time and expertise in helping me get ready," Stacy said. The ladies finished their waffle fries and took a few sips from their sweet tea before they got down to business.

"Let's get right to it, Stacy. thank you for applying for this position. Please give us a brief introduction about your background and experience as well as what makes you interested in this role."

"Sure," Stacy replied. "I grew up in Oklahoma and went to an all-girls high school where I played on-"

"Stop, stop, stop" Joan interrupted. "Too much irrelevant information. Limit your answer to information that is relevant for the role you are interviewing for. You should be prepared to give what's often called an elevator pitch. If you had an opportunity to ride together in an elevator with a potential catering client you'd have just a few moments to describe the key reasons your service is the best and why they ought to call you when they plan their next event. You have a captive audience, but only for a moment. It should be precise and informative. Most of all it needs to be engaging," Joan continued. Stacy was a little embarrassed but felt like she understood what Joan was trying to explain to her.

"Let's begin again with the same question." Joan said.

Stacy began tentatively, "I've been working in the hospitality industry for six years specializing in event planning and hosting. I feel that my specialty has been in providing guest satisfaction to secure repeat business. At the urging of my supervisor and some peers I began to take some classes to make myself more eligible for management roles and I finished my Associates Degree in Business Administration last fall. I think the thing about this role at Powell that most excites me is the ability to leverage the skills of customer service and event hosting in a role that has real meaning for the people it serves." Stacy's response had built momentum as she went. She had a twinkle in her eye as she finished.

Joan was sincerely impressed and told her so. "Much better. This is exactly the kind of introduction that really helps people understand who you are and why you might be a good fit for the organization," Joan said.

Author's note:

Although an Elevator Speech is generally considered a sales tool, it is a useful tool in narrowing down what you might say when you are given just a moment to explain who you are, your key strengths, and how you will add value to an organization. As you get opportunities to practice it you will find a way to describe it that feels natural and genuine. It will be rehearsed but won't sound like a recitation to those you are sharing it with.

Who are you? What statement best describes who you are and what you stand for? A coach might talk about their role to teach teamwork and interdependence, help people raise their expectations of themselves, or some other philosophical value of their craft. Similarly, a Maître' D might explain that his purpose is to ensure guest satisfaction.

Take a few moments to capture your purpose here. Don't worry if it's not perfect or polished. You will revise it as you practice.

_____

_____

_____

_____

_____

_____

_____

_____

_____

What Skills do you have? What education or experiences can you mention that highlight the special skills that make you eligible for this role? A salesman might talk about special sales awards that highlight her ability to meet and exceed sales goals. She should talk about specific things that differentiate her as successful. A teacher might talk about the year she raised AP scores in her Algebra class and how these traits will make her successful in your organization as well. A project manager might talk about how he kept a specific key project on time and under budget. He should also talk about what approach he uses to stand out from the crowd and how these skills transfer to other organizations.

Capture here what skills you have that make you a star in your field and what experience you have had that demonstrates those skills. As stated above, don't worry about making it perfect; you will revise it

over time as you practice. _____

_____

_____

_____

_____

_____

_____

_____

How will you add value to the new organization? Think of this as the
opportunity to attempt to close the sale. You want to explain how
what you've done in your previous roles or your training will help you
to add value right away in the new organization. If you have done your
homework about the company and organization you are applying to,
you know what they need, what their goals and mission are, and what
their weaknesses are. Selling yourself as a solution to their problems
is exactly the purpose of the elevator pitch.

A weather reporter might explain why her ability to help viewers
understand what the forecast means in practical terms will raise

viewership among stay-at-home moms, which is a particular goal of the station. A dental hygienist could explain that her approach with children can help increase the number of families with children on the patient list, just as she had done in her previous practice. An attorney might explain why her ability to speak a certain language creates a sense of comfort with the business leaders the firm is trying to attract.

Capture here how you are going to add value for potential employers.

_____

_____

_____

_____

_____

_____

_____

_____

"Thank you," Joan said," I see from your resume that you have a Microsoft certificate. Please explain how you would send a personalized form letter to all members of a group."

Stacy thought for a moment and explained the steps one would take to capture personalized information in Excel, how the contents of the document would be formatted in Word and how to set up Outlook to process the job. She captured a few notes as she spoke.

Without any hesitation, Joan jumped into her next question, "Tell me how to create a table of contents, an index, and footnotes in Word."

Stacy explained in detail how each of these tasks can be completed from the references tab.

"Very Nice," said Joan with a smile as Stacy finished. "Now let's talk about event planning and hosting. Please describe a successful event you planned and hosted."

Stacy cleared her throat, took a sip and jumped in. "I'd find out how many guests we'll be hosting and the theme of the event." She said, "So, let's assume its 15 people and they're meeting in a boardroom setting. I always make sure to get the list of attendees for the invitations and I work with the sponsor to approve the invitations for the event. Depending on what the requirements of the meeting are, I have a couple of go to caterers I like to use. Go Nuts Do-Nuts has a great continental service they offer and I usually get lunches from the Pat Your Belly Deli."

After being patient, Joan raised her hand to stop Stacy. "Stacy, there are two opportunities here. It's always best to use a real example of what you did do in a situation that matches what is asked for in the question. Also, I very clearly asked for a real example so if you speak in the hypothetical it indicates you weren't listening well."

Stacy was a little flustered. She knew that this candid coaching was going to make a big difference, but that didn't take away the discomfort of being corrected. Joan reminded Stacy of the prep work they had done to document the relevant experiences that might be of value in the interview.

Joan was firm but not unkind. "Remember, this phone screen is all about answering famous interview questions 1 and 2. They want to know you have the education and training to do the job and that you have the ability to perform or learn the duties of this role. Your best way to show you can do it, is to show you have done it."

Joan gave Stacy another chance to discuss the question and they agreed that this was an area that they could spend time rehearsing better.

"Let's spend some more time talking about the kinds of questions that folks will ask in an interview to answer famous interview questions 1 and 2. Some questions are intended to learn about your skills *and* maybe your ambitions or fit for the organization. I'd like to go through a list of some sample questions with you. We may be able to train ourselves to listen for the question behind the question."

Chapter 16

Henry

Sitting in Henry's office after enjoying lunch together at Mean Tony's Pizzeria, Paul and Henry had an uneasy feeling as they reviewed their notes from Lewis Hall's interview. They had the feeling that they might have missed something in the interview. They thought back on a comment Maria made as they made their way back to their offices right afterward. "You should be careful in an interview to challenge your own judgement if you find you love or hate the candidate." They realized, upon reflection, that they had been so impressed with Lewis that they might have been generous in their questioning of him. For example, they remembered that they'd asked him to talk about how he overcame a mishap and what he'd learned from it. As they reviewed their notes they realized they'd let Lewis slide on that part of the question and had possibly gone soft on his Microsoft skills questions.

"We need to write better questions." Paul said. Although they had agreed on what specific skills they required from their successful candidate, they didn't do a very good job of creating the kind of questions that would teach them what they needed to know. They needed to ask questions that were rigorous and challenging to eliminate subjectivity from the process.

Henry spoke up in agreement, "I found some sample questions online that should help us do better. But I think that it's about more than asking questions from a sheet of paper. We need to be sure we're getting to the bottom of what we're trying to learn. After the interview with Lewis, I asked Maria how we did. She scrunched up her eyebrows and said, 'about as well as anyone'. Paul, the way she said it, I'm sure it wasn't a compliment. She said that most people feel successful if they've gotten through their full list of questions and they feel very good if they've made the candidate very uncomfortable." Henry rubbed his chin while he sought the words he should say next. He decided that it would be better if he could get Maria to explain it, so he dialed her number.

"Maria, this is Henry. You are on speaker phone and Paul is here with me," he said. "I was sharing with him some of the information you told me after we interviewed Lewis. Do you mind explaining again what you told me?"

"Oh, Henry, I would love to share my insights but right now is a bad time. I'm late for a meeting. Can we meet in my office at 5:00?" Maria was generous in her manner but it was clear that she really did need to excuse herself.

"Sure," he said as they hung up the phone.

Chapter 17

Henry

As Henry and Paul approached Maria's office at 4:55 they brought with them a box of Samoas® girl scout cookies that Henry had bought from a friend whose daughter was selling them. Maria was still in a meeting with someone else and from what they could hear through the closed door, it was not going well. Ultimately, Maria finished the meeting a few minutes after 5:00 and seemed distracted. The cookies did make a difference in her mood and after a few moments of quiet as they ate cookies together, Maria started the conversation. "In the morning, when you are getting ready for work, do you have the news on in your home?" She looked at Paul and then Henry as she bit into another cookie. Without waiting for a response from either, she said she liked to watch the local newscaster. "Today I was watching," she continued, "and the meteorologist was at the local office of the girl scouts. He was asking a few recent recipients of the Golden Award to explain what the sale of cookies enabled for them personally and for their organization. The girls were very articulate and excited and it was easy to see their enthusiasm for the annual cookie sales.

"The reporter didn't follow up with any questions that stretched the girls or challenged their statements. For example, what if the reporter had asked for the portion of each dollar earned on cookie sales that went to programs built for the girls, or whether there were opportunities to be more inclusive of girls with disabilities?" Henry and Paul both creased their brow as if to indicate the inappropriateness of those kinds of questions.

"The morning news shows are full of these kinds of interviews. If you watch in the evening hour you might see interviews by people like Megyn Kelly, Barbara Walters, Katie Couric, or Anderson Cooper. These Journalists do ask hard questions that get to the truth of a matter."

Paul nodded his head in agreement, "I recently watched Cooper destroy a senator in a professional and calm manner. He's good. The one thing I've noticed about him is that his goal isn't to slay his guests, but he's willing to challenge them for the sake of the truth. People should be very prepared before they go to be interviewed by him."

"Yes," Maria said. "My, we've finished off these cookies. Lucky for us the girl scouts will be happy to sell us more. When we conduct job interviews we should be more like this second group of interviewers than the local reporters we talked about."

"I've seen interview panels where the hiring manager has assembled neat little packets including the resumes, cover letters, six sheets of skill and personality-based questions, and is armed with a carefully built spreadsheet to mathematically identify which candidate is best for the job. They carefully solicit interview panelists from a cross-functional field and assign each category of questions to an interviewer based on some criteria. Sounds good, right?"

Henry spoke right up agreeing with Maria. "I wish I was that organized for this upcoming set of interviews. I can't see anything wrong with what you've described but your tone seems to imply that you are not a fan, Maria. What's up?"

Maria stood up from her desk and walked to the window. Instead of gazing outside, she stooped to get two bottled beers out of her mini-fridge from the Tin Cannon Brewery and brought them over to the men. "Being an organized interviewer and hiring manager is a strength. However, sometimes managers will be so proud of their organized packets and scoring spreadsheet that they act like local morning reporters instead of hard hitting journalists. See what I mean?"

She didn't wait for an answer. "When you interviewed Lewis the other day, what opportunities did you miss to really understand his strengths and qualifications better than you did?'

Paul took a long drink from his bottle as he reached for his notes before he replied. "We've actually discussed what we should have done better in that interview. We let him slip on half-answering some of our questions. Also, it felt like we let him drive the conversation more that we'd have liked."

Maria interrupted, "Did you think Lewis intentionally overlooked parts of your questions with a motive to deceive?"

Paul responded quickly, "I actually thought at the time of the interview that he wasn't a good listener. I think he didn't aim to overlook parts of the question; I think he was just so eager to tell us what he'd prepared for the interview that he looked for openings and just pushed his agenda."

Henry had been listening carefully but now he worried that the conversation was getting away from him. He was the hiring manager for this role and he felt he should show a bit more ownership in this meeting. "We have already started identifying better questions for the other interviews. It makes sense to be sure that we're being aggressive enough."

Maria raised her wrist to look at her watch. By now it was about 6:30 and she was surprised to see how quickly the time had passed. "There is no problem with the questions you asked, at least for the phone screen. What needs to improve is your curiosity about the truth behind the question. If you are asking a question because it's on the interview worksheet without any investment in learning the true answer, you've misunderstood the process. For my money," she said as she stood and pulled her jacket off the hook on the wall, "the most interesting information comes out of the follow-up questions. I need to go now. Thanks for bringing those delicious cookies. Please leave your bottles in my waste basket when you leave. I'll take care of them in the morning." She pulled the belt tight around her waist as she walked out of the office and into the corridor. She walked briskly toward the elevator as she pulled her gloves on. The two men looked at each other with a smile. It was just like Maria to stand up and leave so abruptly.

There was a lot to consider in what Maria had explained. After discussing it for some time, they realized that what they needed was experience. Maybe they could benefit from conducting what some people call mock interviews. It sounded good in theory but they weren't sure how to go about it.

Chapter 18

Stacy

Joan realized that she hadn't been successful in helping Stacy understand what she meant about the famous interview questions and the meanings behind them. They had agreed to meet at the public library in a reading room they reserved for the evening so Joan wanted to prepare something that might illustrate her point in an efficient way that Stacy couldn't misunderstand.

"Thanks for meeting me here," Stacy said to Joan as Joan slowly opened the large wooden door with its oversized window. The hinges moaned slightly under the weight of the swing door as Joan entered the room with her laptop and large bag in tow. Joan pulled a portfolio from her bag. It held a few packets of paper and as Joan opened it up, Stacy saw what looked like a Venn diagram. Joan pulled out two packets and set one in front of herself and handed one over to Stacy. She took a sip from her water bottle and cleared her throat.

"You've heard me speak of The Four Famous Interview Questions," Joan said as she laid her left hand on Stacy's copy of the packet. "I've created a packet that should help in classifying the questions you might encounter in interviews into these questions. I have found that when people struggle in an interview, it's because they tend to misunderstand the purpose of the question."

The Four Famous Questions of Interviewing

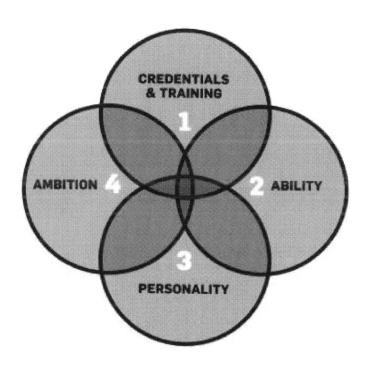

Stacy began to lift the packet but Joan reached out and gently rested her hand on Stacy's wrist, causing her to focus her attention back onto Joan. "Remember, you just have a moment to let them know that you are the best candidate for their role. Just to review, here are the definitions of each question:

1) Do you have the proper education, skills, training, certification and experience to qualify for this job?

2) Do you have the ability to learn to do the job? This includes technical troubleshooting and analytical problem solving.

3) Is your personality a good fit for our company or organization? How well do you navigate interpersonally and how do you react to various social situations?

4) What is your ambition level? To what extent will you stretch yourself in this role and how interested are you in advancement over time?

Questions 1 and 2 are requirements that must be satisfied objectively and questions 3 and 4 are requirements that differentiate the best fit candidates and are a little more subjective.

"Let's open the packet now and take a look at the format I've used to organize the questions," Joan said. "You'll see that I've included questions that are relevant to a variety of jobs and roles. You'll see that some questions may fit into more than one category. As we look at it, I hope it adds value."

Question	Category	How to respond
Explain how Ohms law plays into an amplification circuit.	1	Technical questions require you to relay information you've learned or problems that need solved. If you don't know the answer, talk about how you'd reason through it or determine the answer.
How do you verify zero energy in a gas delivery system?	1	
What is the difference between Mousse and Pudding?	1	
What are the most difficult aspects of Sarbanes-Oxley compliance?	1	
How do you recognize medication seeking behavior?	1	
What is the Roth IRA contribution limit for the current year?	1	
Explain how to make a perfect omelet.	1	
Explain how you have improved sales in your current role.	1	
How do you determine if a vacuum system leak is external or internal?	1	
Explain the scope of your internship/residency/etc..	1	
How do you balance the rights of the accused against public safety?	1	
How do you calculate the appropriate Furnace/AC unit for different sized homes?	1	
What is the appropriate way to set a bicycle seat for a client?	1	
What are the ingredients in a Martini/Margarita?	1	
How can you tell if you should replace or resurface rotors?	1	
Why are manhole covers round?	2	Lots of questions are geared to learning how the candidate thinks about a problem. If you don't know or if the question seems unanswerable, let the panel see how you process information and come up with a response.
How many golf balls would fit into a standard size train boxcar?	2	
How much ice would form on the leading edge of the wing of a 747 at 30000 feet?	2	
Which technology do you wish would play a bigger role in the industry?	2	
How do you know when you have put forth your best work?	3	Questions that seek to understand how you handle a situation may be difficult so buy yourself a moment if needed to think about it. Your answer should take the approach of describing the situation, identifying the obstacles, what action you took, how it turned out and what you might do differently if you have a chance to do it again.
What do your peers say are your strengths?	3	
Do you tend to have better relationships with your superiors, peers or subordinates?	3	
Provide an example of how you've dealt with a conflict in the workplace.	3	
What are our firm's values?	3	
How do you deploy a change you disagree with?	3	
How do you manage competing priorities?	3	
How have you explained to a client that what they want cannot be done?	3	Some questions are designed to understand your personality. Some don't have a right or wrong answer but are designed to understand how well you know yourself or how well you think on your feet.
When have you overstepped your role and how did you resolve the outcome of it?	3	
Describe an interaction where your boss was being unreasonable.	3	
What are you doing to strengthen your weaknesses?	3	Some questions are geared to understand how well you've prepared for the interview by researching the firm.
If you were an animal, which animal would you be?	3	
What is the best advice you've ever received and why?	3	
How have you handled disappointment in your past?	3	
How far have you gone above and beyond to provide excellent customer service?	4	The interviewer wants to know how hard you'll work to succeed in the current job and what your future plans are.
Where do you see yourself in 5 years?	4	

As Stacy and Joan looked at the table that Joan had created, it became clear to Stacy how important it was to understand the question behind the question. Once she understood the true purpose of the question, she felt she could more easily provide the answer they were really asking—and she felt more prepared.

Author's Note: There is an unending list of potential interview questions. It is rare to find one that doesn't fit into one of these four categories unless the motive of the question isn't inspired by a desire to select the right person for the job. Sometimes, unanswerable questions or unnecessarily difficult questions defy categorization. The way to handle these questions is to assume they fall into category two and try to demonstrate how you'd go about finding the right answer.

Please see the appendix for additional lists of questions or consult the internet. Several lists have been published with industry-specific questions. You'll have to review them for yourself and identify which category or categories they represent. Experience placing the questions into these categories can be good practice in preparing for interviews.

Chapter 19

Henry and Stacy

Henry and Paul gathered to do the phone interview of their candidate Stacy Koenig. Maria was unavailable to join them but she had sat with them during several of their phone interviews since the night she let them drink beer in her office. She was convinced that they finally understood what she'd been trying to teach them about getting to the real information behind the question.

Paul handed Henry a green tea that he'd brought for him while Henry dialed the number. As it rang, both men got ready to capture notes for the interview.

"Hello, this is Stacy."

"Hello Stacy, this is Henry Williams calling from Powell United. Is this still a good time to chat?" After she responded that it was, and he informed her that Paul was also on the call, he asked his first question.

"Stacy, can you please give us a little information about your background and let us know why you are interested in this role at Powell?" She couldn't believe that this question was exactly as Joan had posed it.

"Yes," Stacy said with enthusiasm. She knew that the best way to give them a good first impression was to show that she was energetic and had charisma. "I've been working in the hospitality industry for several years and over that time I've had the opportunity to act as a trainer for many people. I found that I had a knack for it. I've honed my skills over time and thought about going into management so I started taking classes on campus nearby and earned my Associate's degree in Business Administration. I happened to see your job posting for this role of assistant coordinator for your emerging leaders program and I saw that it called for a solid mix of my experience and my passion for helping people. I have also been following Powell United since you sponsored a

73

Habitat for Humanity home in my neighborhood. Lots of companies have a slogan but I've rarely seen a company live up to a slogan the way Powell does. If I'm not mistaken it's to 'be good and do good; but if you must choose, be good'." She tried not to overdo it but she remembered Joan telling her it was good to research the company you applied to and even the interviewers if possible. She wanted to demonstrate confidence without taking over the conversation so she stopped right there.

"Thank you," Paul said from the other end of the line. "Can you tell us about some of the classes you took in your education program?"

She was prepared to defend having only an associate degree when a bachelor's was published as a requirement in the posting, but when she thought about what Paul must be asking she decided to discuss the topics from her curriculum that would be most valuable for this role. "The classes I really enjoyed the most," she began, "were business strategy and behavioral theory. Normally people took these classes in succession but because of a scheduling issue I faced, I ended up taking them in the same semester. I felt like these two specific classes gave me visibility into how to identify what the business team needs and how to build a plan to achieve it. I learned how to deploy the plan successfully to people using approaches that make ideas stick and influence lasting change." She was worried about having a longwinded answer but had one more thing she wanted to say. To avoid risking an interruption, she kept going. "My business communication class then helped me identify

74

how to present my ideas in a more formal and professional way in a variety of settings: face-to-face, written, and in a presentation setting to a larger group." She stopped speaking to allow for the next question. Nervously, with her pen, she traced some of the letters on the prep-sheet she had in front of her.

Paul and Henry looked at each other approvingly. She was off to a good start. They turned to their questioning sheets to ensure they gave her the same questions that the other candidates were asked.

"Stacy," Paul broke in. "This is Paul speaking. Please tell us about a time when you were asked to perform a duty that was outside of your normal responsibilities."

Stacy allowed a few seconds of silence to hang in the air to show that she was thinking about the question. She had already thought about that question because of the prep work that Joan had encouraged her to do and she had an answer on the tip of her tongue. "Yes, I'll tell you about the time I had to take over a large catering event without much notice. I was working at the Blue Shark as a food server and had been asked to work on several catering events that we did. We had a very nice seafood buffet service that we provided which was very popular in the spring. We were able to get a lot of business because of a nearby wedding chapel that had a nice room for banquets but no kitchen." She realized she was starting to drift from her message so she quickly turned it back to the point. "Our Catering Manager had agreed to meet the wedding planner for an upcoming event but needed to leave town suddenly for a family emergency. I was able to step up to the opportunity and took over the event to ensure it was a big success." Stacy took a quick inventory of what she'd said so far. She'd explained the situation so she needed to explain the obstacles and how she handled them. "After I met with the wedding planner and began to work with the chef to get everything ordered and planned, the planner called me to let me know that some members of the wedding party had specific allergies and the bride was sensitive about not letting anyone feel awkward about their allergies. I was able to work with the chef to ensure that all dishes were gluten free and that we segregated shellfish onto one end of the table so that we didn't risk any exposure."

"It was my first time managing such a big affair but it all worked out very well. In fact, the sister of the bride was so impressed that she referred us to one of her girlfriends for a wedding in the fall. The Catering Manager wasn't able to return to the restaurant and I was selected to perform her duties. One of the first things I worked out with the chef was to improve the questionnaire we use when setting up events to include questions about food sensitivities before we get too far into the process." She stopped talking and quickly reviewed what information she'd provided. Believing that she'd fully responded she waited quietly for the next question.

Paul asked a follow-up to his original question, "How did you determine that the goal of avoiding any awkwardness among the guests was achieved?"

Stacy hadn't anticipated that question. In fact, since it wasn't part of her scripted response, she stammered just a bit as she looked for the answer. Her answer actually had a more authentic feel to it as she explained that she was able to position herself near the serving line to monitor the proceedings. She noticed after the first few guests came through the line that there was a bit of concern expressed by some guests so she made a sign to more clearly indicate what people could expect. "We have also incorporated the use of signage into our practice to clarify these kinds of situations for our guests."

"Thank you," Paul replied. He had a golden moment then, realizing that he'd gotten to the thing he wanted to know about Stacy and felt strangely proud of that moment of raw honesty in the interview. He'd asked a question that was difficult to anticipate, therefore not easy to script.

Henry and Paul asked Stacy their remaining questions. She did quite well on all the competency questions and seemed to be the kind of person they'd want on their team. They both felt that this had been their most successful interview. They were getting enough practice to start to feel like they could be good at this. As they were getting ready to end the call, Henry asked whether Stacy had any questions. In fact, she did. "Can you tell me about the next steps for your process?"

Henry said, "We expect to make our decision by Friday about which candidates will advance to the on-site interview phase so you should hear back from our HR department by Monday."

Stacy thanked the men. Although she was a little concerned about how long this process had taken already, she felt it wouldn't provide any benefit to mention it so she let it go. "Thank you, I'm looking forward to meeting you in person," she said as they ended the call and hung up the phone.

Chapter 20

Henry

Paul and Henry were seated for lunch at a taco bar. Paul pushed the chips and salsa to the far end of the round table they were seated at, near the window so they'd have a place to lay out their paperwork. The goal of the meeting was to identify their top two candidates to invite for a face-to-face interview. They had completed their phone screens and had captured notes about each candidate. They could have probably done this over email but they were pleased to have an excuse to take the lunch hour away from the office.

"Paul," Henry began, "I'm glad we could get away today for this. I'm anxious to get on to the next stage and I think we can decide quickly who to invite for the face-to-face. I really liked this one here," he said, grabbing a resume, "Stacy Koenig. She seemed to have the right energy level and had solid skills. Also, I liked this other one really well. Larry Kunz has been working as an office manager for several years and might slip into this role quite easily. He's already done most of the things we want our successful candidate to learn." Paul's head was nodding slowly as he enjoyed some chips while listening to Henry. The waitress stopped by to refill their sodas as Paul began to reply.

"Henry, I agree about Stacy but I thought Larry was a little over-confident, like he'd been there, done that. It didn't feel like he was passionate about taking on this role; at least not as much as some of the other candidates. I wanted to talk about Lewis Hall. You know, we were just starting out when we interviewed him and maybe we didn't get as much out of his interview as some of the later ones. Initially I had a feeling that something was off about him but I'm glad I waited to make a decision about him until after all interviews were completed."

"I agree that Stacy, Lewis, and Larry are our leading candidates. The others really couldn't demonstrate that they had the computer skills we need or that they have experience planning and running events." Henry took the resumes for Debbie, Anil, and David to give to their HR partner so they could receive a polite email to let them know they wouldn't be considered further. "I have this spreadsheet Maria gave me to rank the candidates." Henry pulled his tablet from his backpack and cleared a place on the table to set it and show Paul. "Maria warned me that it can be tricky to rely solely on our emotions and memories when choosing our best candidate. I've prepopulated it with the criteria we decided were important for this role."

The two men looked at the spreadsheet and returned to their notes to recollect their assessment of the candidates against the criteria. It was imperative for them to be able to narrow their candidates to two by this afternoon so that they could schedule the travel for the finalists and get them interviewed next week.

The spreadsheet required them to establish a list of criteria and rank them by importance. In the ranking, they were to establish which items were requirements. If any candidate did not possess all requirements, they could not pass on to the next round. The test question they applied to determine if something should be required was "do I expect to mentor someone on this topic or should they just know it?" The remaining qualities were then ranked according to how much of a factor they would play in the candidates' success in the role and how well they predicted a good cultural fit in the organization. The rankings were somewhat subjective and while Paul had certain views about their importance, as the hiring manager Henry had to have the final word on their ranking. After all, Henry had to be sure that he felt comfortable being represented by the person who was selected. Paul and Henry used a 5-point scale for the criteria weighting and a 3-point scale for the assessment. For several of the criteria they had to define what constituted a certain score.

After some discussion and debate they had the full spreadsheet populated on the topics they captured from the screening. They had taken longer than expected but luckily neither had a meeting at the office they needed to hurry back for. They paid their bills and as they put away the paperwork and tablet, Henry was proud of their work and that they were using a proven system to get the best candidate. He reflected on something Paul had said during their discussion. It *would* have been good to have the spreadsheet in hand during the interview. That way they could enter the data in real time rather than relying on their memories and they could refer to the table during the interview to ensure they really had the answer rather than needing to infer it after the fact.

Henry showed Paul the completed schedule on the tablet as they buckled themselves into the car as they prepared to drive back to Powell's campus. "Of course, there are some hidden cells and formulas running in the background to make it look nice but it sure is easy to make the decision with this tool. I'd have said Larry was our strongest candidate and if only he had Mail Merge skills he'd have the highest score. As it is, it looks like we have Stacy and Lewis as our finalists. I'll show our table to Maria and have a rejection notification sent to Larry."

Candidate		Lewis Hall		Stacy Koenig		Larry Kunz	
		Raw Score	Weighted score	Raw Score	Weighted score	Raw Score	Weighted score
Criteria	Weighting						
Software skills							
Mail Merge	5	3	15	3	15	0	0
Outlook	5	3	15	3	15	3	15
Powerpoint multimedia integration	5	3	15	3	15	3	15
Excel Macro creation	5	3	15	3	15	3	15
Microsoft Project task creation	3	3	9	1	3	3	9
Event Planning							
Experience in coordinating logistics	5	3	15	3	15	3	15
Experience in guestlist management	5	3	15	3	15	3	15
Dealing with difficult people	3	3	9	3	9	3	9
Presentation experience							
Formal or informal settings (1-Toastmaster or coursework, 2-lead instruction, 3-present to managers)	3	2	6	1	3	3	9
Technical complexity of material	3	2	6	1	3	2	6
Size of audience (1-intimate <5 2-small group <15 3-large group>15)	4	2	8	3	12	2	8
Other							
Customer service	3	2	6	3	9	3	9
Management of conflicting priorities	3	2	6	3	9	2	6
Get it done mentality	4	3	12	3	12	3	12
All musts met?		yes	152	yes	150	no	143

Chapter 21

Henry

"Well, how hard is it to learn mail merge?" Maria said to Henry over the phone. He was driving home at the end of the day and realized he'd missed Maria at the office but didn't want to delay any further the discussion of finalizing the candidates. He'd called her on her cell phone to let her know about his decision to invite Stacy and Lewis to the campus for interviews. The tone of her question was a little impatient as she asked whether Henry thought Larry should be disqualified over the lack of one specific skill. Henry was frustrated, and a little ticked off. Now he was glad he was having this conversation over the phone. He knew that his body language would have betrayed him in this moment. "Actually, we were focused on ensuring we narrowed it down to two people and we followed the process you taught us."

Maria could hear the frustration in his voice so she was more careful as she continued. "I'm about to drive through the woods and sometimes lose a call when I do so let me get to the point quickly," she said, taking a mental note of her tone. "If you think Larry is just as strong as the other candidates with this one gap that can be easily overcome we can probably override the guidance of just having the top two candidates come for the face-to-face interview." She realized she'd been misunderstood as overly critical earlier but hoped that the extra context she was providing might ease Henry's reaction.

"Yes," Henry said after a brief moment of silence. "I think it would be good to bring all three candidates for face-to-face interviews. Why don't I bring the worksheet with me to your office in the morning? You can help me through the next steps." He was about to wish Maria a pleasant evening and hang up but something told him he should extend gratitude. "Maria, I appreciate all the time you have spent with me on this process. I know that your expertise and experience are speeding up my learning. Thank you for your help. Have a good evening, I'll see you tomorrow."

Maria was pleased to hear Henry express his gratitude. She knew she could come on strong and she *was* becoming impatient with this particular project. She respected Henry and knew that with continuing training and mentoring she could help bring him further along. She said goodnight and hung up the phone as she approached the turn into the woods. As she rounded the bend and over the old stone bridge into the county Maria's thoughts remained on Henry. She was impressed at his ability to learn and his quick response to feedback. She found herself being a little impatient when he didn't catch on quicker to things that were fairly natural to her. At these times, she reasoned, she needed to remind herself that she'd had the benefit of several years' experience. In fact, if she were honest about it, she'd made many of the same errors that she was seeing Henry make. She determined that she would do what she could to ensure Henry's future was strong.

Chapter 22

Henry

Paul and Henry decided to get together to watch a baseball game at Henry's home. With their Tin Cannon beers in hand, they entered the apartment. Paul turned on the TV and found the channel with the game while Henry fed his tropical fish. He checked for a moment to see that his new butterfly fish was schooling with the angelfish before he turned his attention to getting a bag of potato chips and joining Paul on the sofa.

The Washington Nationals were playing well, but the attention of the two men drifted away from the game. Over the next two days they would interview their three candidates and finally make a decision about filling the position.

"Henry, we've really covered the skill-based competencies in our phone interviews. I understand that we may wish to press the candidates on their skills but the final two of the famous questions are all about how the personality of the candidate fits into the type of organization you are trying to build. I guess I didn't really think about it before now but I'm curious about your vision for the future of your organization. I imagine that this assistant will be merely the first of many additions to your organization as you continue at Powell," Paul said as Henry was watching a double play at home plate.

Paul opened another beer and looked at Henry who responded, "Paul, I'm mostly interested in hiring someone who is competent and honest. We need to hire someone who fits into the culture of Powell United so that we can influence the leaders of the company." He paused as he thought of what other qualities he'd like in an employee. "I suppose that this person will be my right hand and eventually might be able to take over my role so that I can move on to other endeavors. If I think of it this way I need to be assured of their loyalty to me and the company and it should be someone I genuinely enjoy being with."

"That makes sense to me," Paul replied. "Some of these qualities might be more difficult to assess but I agree about the direction you are going with it. I also want to tell you about a TED talk I listened to that might give some insight into how we pose these kinds of questions. Adam Grant, an organizational psychologist and professor at Wharton's, gave a talk entitled 'Are You a Giver or a Taker?' In it Dr. Grant reveals that the most successful people are the givers and that organizations comprised mostly of givers and no takers are more creative and collaborative, more efficient

Figure 2. Are you a giver or a taker?

and productive. One key point he makes is that introducing a giver into an organization of takers will have no positive impact but introducing just one taker into an organization of givers will have a strong negative impact." Paul paused and took a few sips from his beer before continuing. "When I heard this speech, I thought about an organization I used to belong to where we had several takers destroy the team culture and eventually the morale of each individual, driving several core team members away. Dr. Grant explains in his talk how he'd discern if someone is a giver or taker. He'd ask this specific interview question: 'Can you give the names of four people whose careers you have fundamentally improved?' The positions of the people cited tells a lot about the direction of the person's influence. Are they sucking up and kicking down or are they reaching out to those with less power to provide a lift up?"

Paul finished his explanation just as the Nats drove in another home run to seal the game. The men both sat quietly as their minds absorbed the concepts Paul had shared.

Chapter 23

Henry

The next morning Larry Kunz was escorted to the conference room where a chilled water bottle had been set out for him. He sat at the head of a dark wooden table with three chairs on each side. Canvas photographs of local landmarks were hung in the room. In just a moment four people gathered at the doorway as the clock showed it was about two minutes before 8:00. The first man introduced himself to Larry as Paul and confirmed that he was indeed one of the men he'd already met on the phone. "And this is Henry who was also on the call," Paul said as he gestured toward Henry. As Henry and Paul settled themselves in the large leather chairs opposite each other and nearest to Larry, Maria extended her hand, leaning forward across the table, introducing herself then turning to introduce Lucas. Lucas had been a mentor to Henry and was renowned across the company for his interviewing prowess. Maria had cashed in a favor with Lucas to attend the interview. There was no illusion that this role required Lucas' particular discernment, but in keeping with Maria's desire to propel Henry as far as possible, she asked Lucas to participate. She had informed Henry that Lucas would be there but had not let him know why. She wanted to allow Henry to do his best without the pressure of feeling like he was being tutored.

"Larry, Thanks for joining us today" Henry began, "although Paul and I met you on the phone, for the benefit of Maria and Lucas would you spend a moment telling us about your background?"

Larry was careful to look around the room and make deliberate eye contact as he began. His notebook was open on the table in front of him and he'd taken a sip of his water. He had copies of his resume, written summaries of previous projects he'd worked on and several pages of handwritten notes. "Thank you for inviting me to your beautiful campus. I couldn't help noticing the pond near the parking lot as I came in and had a moment to read the signage about your commitment to the environment and the local community." All four interviewers looked down at their papers uncomfortably as Larry appeared to be preparing to ramble on. Fortunately, he got to the point and gave a brief history of his education and experience including his current position as an office manager for the local office of a global consulting company. "I have found a lot of satisfaction in providing my manager maximum freedom by taking upon myself many mundane duties, which allows her to focus her energy on the things that only she can do. While we've worked together she's been able to publish several key essays that have shaped policy across the company and I feel like I've enabled that. I'd like to add that same level of value to Henry in this organization so that he can focus his energy on building the program."

"Thank you, Larry," Henry said. "The organization you've been in is significantly larger than ours and it sounds like you've had the ability to add a great deal of value. What is your motivation for pursuing our position?"

Larry looked at his water bottle for a moment before speaking. "The organization I'm in has grown and expanded around me and my duties have grown in magnitude but not really in importance. I feel like maybe I haven't grown much over the last year or so either. I'd like to bring my expertise and experience to Powell and try to grow my career and influence in the company. I've heard so many things about the company and I feel like it's a good place to grow."

After the interviewers captured their thoughts on Larry's response Paul began to ask a question when Lucas gently held up his hand to stop him. "And...what *have* you learned about our company?" Lucas said. Henry noticed that Lucas hadn't captured any notes and that his pen was laying on his unopened notebook on the desk. The cap was still on, almost as if to indicate Lucas didn't expect to take many notes. Lucas' body language was also different than Henry had seen in the past. He kept his hands on the table, often folded together and rather than facing perpendicular to the table with his chair and body, he was oriented toward Larry. He looked more toward the candidate than at him and only made eye contact when asking a question. Henry was amazed at this posture and approach. The crowd waited quietly until Larry could respond. Henry and Paul both noticed that Lucas didn't feel the slightest obligation to fill the silence that he'd created nor did he allow Larry off the hook about the question.

"I learned that Powell has a variety of products that are created across the company, and overseas, to increase the power of education and to be used in schools, business, and even in government agencies and across a wide variety of disciplines. I read an article published by the chamber of commerce on the importance of leadership development and your speech to the chamber," he said, gesturing toward Henry. "I also think I remember your slogan. It's about being and doing good." While Henry expected Lucas' question was intended to make Larry more nervous, Lucas' body language seemed to put Larry at ease and after overcoming the shock of being asked an off-script question, he did seem to answer with ease.

As Paul looked back to his scoring sheet there was no place to write the information he wanted to capture about this answer so he had to write in the margin. Undaunted, he posed his first question about the details of hosting a workshop with 18 people who were not known to him and how he'd organize and facilitate the event. Larry answered this question with ease and several follow-up questions on specific logistical details didn't yield any new information.

Henry was very interested in Lucas' behavior. He didn't seem bored or impatient but he wasn't overly engaged in Paul's question, or Larry's answers either. He was polite as he took several quiet sips from the coffee he brought in an insulated cup with the Powell logo on it.

Maria asked Larry what his biggest strength was. Larry spoke about his ability to be organized and efficient in a way that gave him more bandwidth to provide for the organization. Her follow up questions allowed him to discuss his methods for keeping himself well organized which included a somewhat complicated mix of tracking actions in a notebook, in Microsoft Project, and in a SharePoint list. While it seemed to work for him, it sounded like it required more overhead and required others to adjust their approach to avail themselves of his services.

Just as Maria was about to move on to another question, Lucas held up his hand gently. "It sounds like your approach to being more efficient, creates a barrier to group efficiency. If you were asked to change the system you've described to optimize the efficiency of the organization, what changes would you make, and how would you deploy them so that the changes would be successful?" Lucas calmly asked.

Henry was impressed at Lucas' skill. The question was asked in a way that didn't intimidate Larry but it was the result of a different kind of listening. Larry was caught off guard but not defensive. He thought for a moment about different techniques he might try and tools he could build to ease the transition to a new method so that it would stick. He also spoke for a moment about how he'd measure the improvement to efficiency in the organization to verify that the changes had been worth it. When Larry had finished, Lucas smiled gently and said, "Thank you," without having raised his pen once.

The interview continued like this for about 30 minutes more until the questioning began to settle down. Henry was watching the clock and knew that they should give Larry a moment to ask them any question he had on his mind. As he looked around the room, he made eye contact with each panelist prior to asking Larry if he had any questions. Lucas, who had been mostly quiet with the exception of his gentle follow-up challenges, gave Henry a look that indicated that he did have another question before they wrapped up.

"Larry, I've really enjoyed this interview with you and I have just one more question for you," Lucas began. "You said in your opening statements that your current firm seems to have grown and expanded while your own career has stagnated. Why do you think that is and what do you think you could have done to change it?" Maria, Henry and Paul all looked at Lucas as he finished his question, wondering where it came from. Lucas didn't return their gaze, he just looked at Larry and waited patiently.

Larry contemplated for a few moments before answering. "I think what happened was that I saw my role as being the chief facilitator for the department. I would always ask myself, 'How can I lift the burden of

Amber?' my manager." A smile stretched across his face as he joked, "I guess I got myself typecast. Really, I think because my thinking was flawed about what I had to offer, people just began to see my value as being restricted to certain types of roles. I guess to fix that I could have changed the way I think about it to 'what does the department need that I can provide?' If I did this I might see opportunities to support tasks that go beyond logistics and share my ideas about other facets." Larry's thoughts seemed to drift. The interviewers watched him in awe as he seemed to have an epiphany about how to fix his career.

"Thank you, Larry." Lucas said as he picked up his pen and set it in his breast pocket. He was done. They concluded the interview and the gentleman from HR came to pick up Larry and escort him back to the lobby.

Lucas stood up and held his notebook and coffee cup against his chest with his left hand. He looked at Henry and Paul then glanced at Maria. "Thank you for inviting me to your interviews. Is our next session at 1:00? Is it also in this same room?" Lucas asked. After confirming these details, he excused himself and quietly left the room in his usual confident way.

Henry couldn't believe what he had witnessed. He looked at Maria who could read his facial expression easily. "Yes, He's got a remarkable way, hasn't he?" she said. Henry had to rush off to a 9:00 meeting that he was already going to be late for so he walked quickly but somewhat in a fog. Luckily the meeting was an update meeting where he was a consumer and he didn't need to prep or present anything for it. He entered the room as quietly as he could and made eye contact with his friend Shane as he found a seat along the wall. Since he wasn't a decision maker in this meeting, he felt like it was ok to let his mind wander about what he'd seen from Lucas.

What did Lucas do differently? Henry thought. Lucas had not studied the questions or reviewed the scoring sheet. In fact, while it seemed that Lucas had not done any homework at all, it was he who was best able to get to the core of what kind of a candidate Larry was. In fact, Larry even seemed to learn a bit about himself. *It must come back to the four famous interview questions,* he finally concluded. Lucas seemed to specialize in trying to understand more about a person than the normal questions reveal.

Chapter 24

Henry

As Henry headed back toward his desk he sent Paul a SMS message to see if he could stop by Paul's desk prior to lunch. Paul responded that it should be fine. He was just finishing some travel expense report approvals and he was eager to speak to Henry.

"I'm still spellbound," Henry said to Paul. He smiled as he thought about it.

Paul agreed, "I've heard Lucas was a legend but now I understand why. Do you think we could ever be that good?" Standing quietly as they contemplated that thought they suddenly snapped themselves out of it. "Let's head down to the cafeteria. I hear they have a curried chicken special today," Paul said as he stood and they started walking down the hall toward the cafeteria. Along the way, they passed Henry's desk and he dropped off his things and grabbed his wallet. They stood in line and got their lunches and found a quiet place in the cafeteria to sit and discuss the interview. About 15 minutes into their meal, they saw Lucas coming into the cafeteria by himself. They saw him get a cup of freshly cut fruit and a small tossed salad. As he came by the cashier, the two men waved him over, hoping to get his attention and hoping he'd be willing to sit with them.

"Hey fellows, how are you doing?" Lucas said showing his perfect white teeth as he smiled at them. He was a very handsome and rugged man with a perfect tan. Normally, he was in a different league than Paul and Henry, but because they were doing this interview together, they felt emboldened to speak to him more casually than normal. Also, they knew of his willingness to provide mentoring and guidance. "Do you think Larry is going to turn it around?" Lucas asked while lifting a forkful of melon to his lips; making eye contact with them. Paul and Henry legitimately didn't know what Lucas meant and it was obvious based on their facial expressions. "You know," he continued, "at his current firm."

Finally, Henry spoke, "What do you mean?" He took a sip of his lemonade through the straw while he waited for Lucas to explain himself.

"Oh, I'm sure he's not going to be your successful candidate. He doesn't have what you are looking for. I just hope he takes to heart the changes he should make to become successful and happy in the job he has," Lucas stated calmly while reaching for a sip of his juice.

If Lucas wasn't expressing any emotion, Henry started to feel some emotion creeping in. *How could Lucas just show up without doing any homework on the position or the candidate and decide so quickly, before even meeting the other candidates, that Larry wasn't the right one for us?* It seemed arrogant of him but Henry had to remind himself of the magic he'd just seen in the conference room. Maybe he just needed Lucas to explain to him what he and Paul were missing.

"You have to keep your lens fixed and focused," Lucas said. "The reason Larry is 'stuck' in the role of an office manager is because that's the right role for him. He's adding value and he's an essential part of the team. I happen to believe that he's in the right role for his skills and experience. In fact, he may be one of the best candidates for an office manager role I've met. But, are you hiring an office manager? If you wanted someone to just run the logistics of your organization, you'd have created the position posting much differently. I studied it before I came to the interview so I understand your vision of the role. More importantly I also have a vision for the right candidate for the role."

Paul had some questions now. "How can you disqualify one of the candidates when you haven't met the other two yet?" Henry nodded his agreement with the challenge. Since Lucas hadn't met the other candidates yet, he had no way of knowing if they were any better at all.

"Ok, I get your point," Lucas responded. "If you had 10 bad candidates, would you feel obligated to put a bad candidate into the role, say the least bad candidate? I would never want to hire someone for a role that is either poorly suited for the role or for whom the organization is a bad fit, even if that meant leaving the position vacant while I looked for additional candidates." Paul had been a supervisor for many years and had received several new employees that had been selected for him but who might have been selected as the least bad candidate. Lucas' words resonated with him as he considered them for a moment.

"The best thing we can offer Larry today is some tools and perspective about how to get what he wants from the job he has. If he's able to succeed with the approach we led him to in the interview he could get what he really wants out of a job he's already good at without the pain of having to move to a new company. Also, I was worried that his biggest strength was in creating systems that made the department inefficient. The position you are hiring for has the opportunity to influence behavior in all departments on campus and I'd hate to sub-optimize the whole system so that your little part might be optimized." Lucas said this with a big grin so that the two could see that he was just ribbing them a bit and not trying to provoke them.

"Look guys, it's like this. I just have a few rules. Maria has told me that she's taught you about the Four Famous Interview Questions. I figure that by the time you've brought them to the face-to-face interview you've already verified, for the most part, that they have the proper education, training, certification and experience to do the job, and that they have the ability to learn the job. In fact, those are so easy to verify that I tend to spend very little time on those two questions. I spend the majority of my time trying to identify whether someone is a good fit for the company, for the organization, for the role, and for their potential new peers. I know you don't like that I mentally dismissed Larry so quickly but tell me honestly. Henry, I know you are looking for a right-hand person who can help you build this organization and who can grow to become your replacement one day. Is Larry that guy?"

Henry stammered a little. He was surprised at how well it seemed that Lucas had read his thoughts. Finally, Henry admitted that Larry was not that guy. As capable as he seemed with many of the tasks he wanted someone to own for the team, he wasn't a good fit for the organization or for Henry. Paul had remained a bit aloof from the conversation until now.

"I'm following what you are saying," Paul finally said, "but I have a different question. I've always heard that it makes sense to keep the candidate on their toes and make them as nervous as you can so that you'll learn how well they handle stress. But you made the candidate so comfortable. Your way is almost soothing. Why is that?"

Lucas was pleased at the desire of these two men to learn and he wanted to provide them a serious response that was helpful. They were running out of time before they had to collect their items to prepare for their next interview together. He decided to give them a direct answer. "Yes, there are times when I want to make the candidate nervous or catch them in a stressful situation but those tend to be brief, intentional moments designed to challenge something they've said or to add a new degree of complexity to a scenario we've described for them. In general, however, I like to get a candidate's best face. If I only have about an hour to learn as much as possible about a person, why would I make it the worst hour of their week? Some people who are great employees suffer from anxiety in an interview setting. Why should I disqualify them because of a situation that says more about me than it does about them? I want to see how well someone does at their best so that I can know what to expect from them day to day. By the way, I like to have my team performing at their best too, so I tend to try to put them at ease, in general, unless there is reason to apply pressure. Now, we need to leave or we'll be late for the interview and it will leave Lewis and Maria alone in the conference room. That won't set either one of them at ease." They all laughed as they stood to throw away their garbage and set their trays in the stack.

Chapter 25

Henry

The interview panelists were all in their seats, ready for the interview, although Paul was a little winded since he'd stopped to use the restroom on the way and had to jog to make it on time. Shortly, Lewis Hall was introduced to the interviewers and took his place at the head of the table. As he had with Larry, Henry invited Lewis to introduce himself and describe his background. Lewis began to explain his role as office manager for the accounting department within the college of business. He explained many of his roles in great detail until the panelists had all set down their pens and it was obvious they had stopped paying attention. Lucas, however, had the same posture he'd taken with Larry. His hands were gently folded together as he looked toward, although not at, Lewis. Henry's attention actually was on Lucas now instead of Lewis. After a few minutes of allowing Lewis his leash, Lucas held his hand up in that now familiar way and interrupted Lewis. "Thank you, Lewis. At the end of a day or week, how do you know if you've made a difference?"

The question startled Lewis as well as Paul and Henry. It certainly stopped the train of thought, if you could call it that, Lewis had been on and caused him to stop and really consider the question. "Well," Lewis began to reply, "Our department has a mission to fulfill and I consider myself to be an important key to our success in that mission so I've created a kind of personal mission statement that I can use to measure myself against. There are two questions I like to think about. I ask myself whether I've furthered the work of the department, the college and the university and I also ask myself whether I've helped prepare any student to make a difference for their family, for their community, and for their chosen field. Since I was young I've found great value in meditation and journaling and so I can usually tell you on a daily or weekly basis what wins I've had. It's weird you would ask me that because mostly people want to measure your value by your title or income. I believe there are lots of ways to add value and I try to look for them."

It was clear to Paul now that what he'd perceived about Lewis in the phone screen was also evident in the face-to-face interview. What he couldn't overlook was that despite Lewis' long-windedness, Lewis had a rare perspective about adding value and measuring success that was consistent with Powell's culture. Lucas had worked his magic again and helped bring out the essential kernel of information to truly illuminate a topic. He'd helped Lewis transcend the mundane minutia of his role, where he was keenly successful, and portray it as a self-actualizing mission.

Henry noticed Paul also looking at Lucas who still hadn't opened his notebook to capture any notes. Lucas was listening to the next question

Maria had asked with an almost passive posture. Maria had a question for Lewis about his classroom presentation style. They had already determined that Lewis was very proficient with software systems and meeting logistics. Lewis was speaking about how his best classes were those where he facilitated discussions rather than classes where he lectured. He really enjoyed the free flow of ideas among different people and he felt he had a way of getting quiet people to contribute and loud people to allow others to talk.

Lucas waited for Lewis to stop speaking and confronted him directly. "Lewis, let's be honest here. You have a style that is long-winded and frankly, doesn't seem to get to the point quickly. I understand that you enjoy the free flow of a facilitated discussion but what feedback have you received from participants in your meetings?" Henry was shocked at Lucas' bluntness. It was a challenge to be sure and Lewis was on the defensive. Lewis paused for a moment and drank about a third of his water bottle while he regulated his emotions and thought of what to say next. To be fair, this was consistent with feedback he'd received from colleagues and even his wife.

"I guess I get pretty excited about a topic and sometimes don't realize when my interest in discussing something outlives other people's interest in hearing about it," Lewis said, not quite defensively but somehow sounding defeated.

Lucas quickly changed his tone now, "If you have received feedback about this before, please tell us what you have been doing to overcome this tendency." Henry was surprised to see Lucas pivot so easily and quickly from such a strong challenge to a more measured approach.

Lewis was visibly uncomfortable in that moment and Paul felt badly for him. In fact, he wondered if he shouldn't have done a better job in the phone screen to prevent this moment from happening. Not to spare Lewis from the discomfort but to avoid wasting the time of the panelists and money spent to bring Lewis to town for the interview. While he was having these thoughts, Lewis began to speak. "I suppose that it stems from my passion for certain topics. It seems that I get so focused on what I want to say and I lose track of the audience and their engagement. I have been reading articles about how to better gauge body language to know when to solicit input. I even joined Toastmasters International to get feedback and it has helped quite a bit. I think I'm nervous today so I apologize for having rambled on."

Lucas treated him gracefully. "I appreciate your sincerity Lewis, I'm quite impressed, actually, with your passion and I think you can find great success if you can remember you are speaking to *PEOPLE* about *YOUR MESSAGE* instead of blasting your message, bombarding the people." Lucas let his words rest in the air as he gave Lewis extended eye contact that expressed support and compassion.

This was clearly a disruptive moment in the interview and Paul wasn't sure how the interview could go on but Maria broke the silence with her next question.

Lewis had pulled it together and was skillfully able to describe to what extent he'd go to ensure success and what level of sacrifice he felt was appropriate to advance the needs of the organization. In fact, if you excluded the awkward portion of the interview, it was a pleasure to be a part of.

"Too bad about the truck crash in the middle of the interview," Henry said to the others after Lewis had been excused from the room after the interview. "I found myself rooting for him. It's a shame, really," Henry said as he put his paperwork under his arm to leave the room.

"Why is that?" Lucas asked. It didn't sound like a challenge but Henry made quick eye contact with Paul. He realized he was about to be educated.

"Who do you know at Powell that has more passion for the work they do and an understanding of the bigger picture than the man you just met?" Lucas turned and looked deeply into the eyes of Maria, Paul and Henry one by one as if to add punctuation to what he'd just said. After allowing that statement to sink in, Lucas continued. "There's no doubting that Lewis has a weakness for being verbose. Is that something we can mentor him on? And if we can help him with this, how far might his passion drive your efforts?" Henry honestly considered the position Lucas was taking about this candidate. "Although we didn't ask about it," Lucas continued, "I believe he'll be fiercely loyal to you, Henry, and to the company. I'd hate for a bad moment of the interview to disqualify someone who could be an excellent team member."

Lucas had made his point and he let silence carry his words into the hearts of the other three as he gathered his items and began to move toward the door. "Our last interview is at 9:00 tomorrow morning, is that right?" After Henry confirmed it, Lucas disappeared into the corridor and toward his next meeting.

Chapter 26

Stacy

Stacy had arrived in her hotel room in the early evening on the day prior to her interview. She was happy that the phone screen had gone well and that she'd been invited to the campus for a face-to-face interview. Travel accommodations had been smooth and her hotel was quite a nice suite in a grand hotel just down the road from the campus. It was a little early to go for dinner so she decided to call her friend and mentor, Joan.

"Hello Stacy," Joan said as she answered the phone. "It's good to hear from you. How was your travel?" After a few minutes of pleasantries, the ladies turned their conversation to the topic of the interview.

"Remember," Joan jumped in, "They invited you to meet with them. This is an exciting step forward. I'd like to remind you of a couple of things we've discussed before. While its normal for the candidates to be nervous and anxious in the interview, you must remember that the company has a need and they are hoping you can fill their need. As you go into the interview, keep in mind, it's your opportunity to sell them on your ability to fill their need. In other words, they'll be lucky to have you. Your job in the interview is to remember that and to sell them on your skills. They must see it to some extent already. They invited you to meet them in person, after all." Stacy was writing a few notes as she listened to Joan's words of wisdom.

"Another point I want to remind you is that some questions are weird. They might ask you something like 'if you were any animal, which would it be?' I believe that questions like this are intended to pull you off your scripted responses and get you to be a little more authentic. If you have a question that seems unusual to you, I recommend thinking again about the four famous questions. If you have to think about being some kind of animal, which animal possess the traits that best exemplify your own characteristics, in a way that helps the panel see how you 1) meet the educational, certification, training and experience requirements of the role, 2) possess the ability to learn and master new skills through training and coaching, 3) represent a good personality fit for their organization and 4) demonstrate an appropriate level of ambition to succeed in this and future roles. Take a moment to collect your thoughts if needed but be careful to remain confident, maintain your energy, and keep your composure."

There was a moment of quiet from Joan's end of the phone. Stacy listened to see if the call had dropped but she thought she heard a slight sigh as Joan was thinking about one more hint she wanted to share. "Stacy, I hesitate to mention this but I think I should. We spoke quite a bit about the interview preparation we do to be sure that we have our talking points we want to be ready with. I want to warn you to keep these in your mind but beware of the trap that politicians fall into." Stacy wasn't sure what she meant at first but remained quiet and listened for her to elaborate. "Have you ever noticed when some politicians are being interviewed by the media how obvious it is that the question being asked doesn't even get heard? A reporter or news anchor will ask a question which appears to simply be a prompt for the politician to spin and launch their script on a tangentially-related topic. It's off-putting and blatantly obvious when it occurs. The reality is that you may have an opportunity to get that message out; either as a response to an upcoming question or at the close of the interview. Even if you can't make your point, don't fret and don't force it."

Stacy understood what Joan was saying and acknowledged her advice. They concluded their conversation and wished each other well before hanging up. Stacy took a moment to freshen up and headed out for a light dinner.

She'd heard a great deal about a local sandwich shop so she decided to try it out. Since she was new to town and hadn't eaten there before she struck up a conversation with the woman behind the counter. She asked what the specialty of the shop was. Since the shop wasn't busy, after placing her order the two ladies continued to chat while her sandwich was being prepared. Stacy noticed that the woman was exceptionally pleasant and seemed quite happy. Finally, Stacy couldn't contain her observation and made mention of how bubbly she seemed. "Oh, I just love my job and helping people. You know to some people I just submit your sandwich order and process your payment but I think about it differently. I think I'm providing the opportunity to enjoy the very best sandwiches available in the city. I'm like a sandwich evangelist." Both women smiled and giggled but Stacy could see that it wasn't a joke. This woman was genuinely happy. "What brings you to our city?" she asked Stacy.

"I'm interviewing for a position at Powell United in their Emerging Leaders department," Stacy replied with confidence.

"Is it a good company to work for?" the sandwich evangelist asked.

"I hope so," Stacy said as she reached for the tray being extended with her beautiful meal.

"Just remember," the lady told Stacy, "The interview is as much an opportunity for you to find out if the company is a good fit for you as it is a chance for them to find out if you are a good fit for them. When I found this company, I was so impressed by their mission and purpose, demonstrated by true actions, that I felt I had to be a part of it. I'm happier in my job than anyone I know. Good luck in your interview. I hope for your happiness."

Chapter 27

Stacy

It was a bright, sunny morning. Stacy awoke in the hotel room with an excitement about her interview scheduled in a few hours. After her conversation at the sandwich shop she thought a great deal about how she was as much responsible as Powell was for ensuring that the relationship between them would be a good fit. She felt that the phone screen had given her more insight into the interviewers and the firm. She decided that after the continental breakfast offered by the hotel she would do a review of the company's values and mission and identify a few questions she'd ask if given an opportunity. She needed to hurry a little to keep herself on schedule. She'd also review her interview worksheet to refresh her mind on the topics she was preparing to speak on and the answers she'd prepare to give. Her excitement had created difficulty sleeping overnight but the fresh strawberries gave her energy and clarity of thought.

Stacy arrived at the beautiful Powell United campus about 20 minutes before the interview was scheduled. She was quite impressed at the beauty of the grounds and structure that housed the company she was hoping to work for. It was not lost on her how different this job would be from where she'd worked previously in the hospitality industry, but she also knew that her skills would be portable and that she'd be able to perform this role. She felt some nerves as she walked across the parking lot to enter the lobby and received her visitors badge in preparation for the interview.

She was escorted from the lobby to a conference room where three men and a woman were already seated. They rose to greet her and she shook hands and made eye contact with each one as she made her way to her seat at the head of the table. She saw that a bottle of water had been placed out for her and she took a moment to situate herself. She took a sip of her water and looked around offering copies of her resume to the interviewers. Each waived it off so she set them beneath her opened notebook. She gave them a calm look that indicated she was set and ready. Henry invited her to introduce herself and describe her background.

"Thank you for inviting me to your beautiful campus," she began. "I have worked in the hospitality industry for several years and there I learned the value of serving the customer, and considering everyone as a customer." As she said this, Henry recalled learning during his MNP experience about Mr. Powell's view of all team members as interdependent customers. "I have had the opportunity to work as a food and beverage server and I also had the opportunity to develop some management skills as a catering captain and catering manager. I learned that I enjoyed working with clients to create their special event, getting all the details right and enabling their vision. I guess the final point I'd like to make is that when I reflected on it I realized how much I liked training and guiding others to be their best selves. I took classes and was able to get my Associates in Business Administration to learn more about how businesses work and to enable me to pursue some leadership opportunities." She felt good about her answer and saw that three of the panelist were taking notes. The fourth panelist didn't even have his pen out and had the most curious posture. He was kind of looking toward her rather than at her and he held his hands together on the table, resting on his closed notebook. He had a beautiful bronze tan and a wonderful gleaming smile. Although he didn't have an intense look about him, he didn't seem distracted or aloof. He appeared to be listening to her response but provided no visual cues to let her know how well her answers were being received.

"Thank you, Stacy," Paul said to her. "Please tell us about an experience you've had when you had more to do than could be done at once. How did you deal with the crisis and how has it changed the way you approach your work?" Stacy thought about the question for just a moment and decided to speak about the time she managed the new year's party for the state senate organization. She took several minutes to explain that she'd been asked to take the lead role of managing the event. She reserved the convention center, took the food order, and organized the DJ and beverage service. Everything went smoothly and as the day approached, all seemed in order but the guest list kept growing along with the number of special requests. "Finally, I realized that I needed more help to ensure that the party would be a very successful and memorable event for the local lawmakers and their friends and families. Luckily, I was able to get sufficient support in time to avoid any risk of failure. I guess what I learned was that I needed to think differently about how to measure success and when to ask for help. I realized that my old way of thinking was to consider efficiency and how to get the most from a conservative amount of resources. I changed my thinking to consider the outcome as a success measure and allocate resources in an effective way to ensure success."

As she stopped speaking she looked at Paul to see if she'd satisfied his question. It seemed she had. She noticed Lucas opening his note pad and was surprised to see the other three interviewers take notice of it. She thought she perceived a slight slow nod from Lucas as he laid his pen down on his opened notebook.

The others were watching Lucas to see if he had a follow-up question, but he didn't seem to have any. Maria was next to ask her question which was about her public speaking experience. Stacy was happy to talk about joining Toastmasters International and how that organization had helped her to think about how to prepare a presentation as well as providing her the opportunity to practice giving speeches and presentations. The club she belonged to was fairly large so she had frequent opportunities to speak to crowds of up to 30 people at a time. She valued the practice of giving and receiving feedback and eventually volunteered to be an officer in her local club. "I found that helping to run the club as an officer," Stacy explained, "provided me a unique opportunity to spend some energy and time to think about how to manage and motivate a group of people. Some of our success came from ideas I was introduced to in my behavioral theory class that I took at the college." Stacy was winding down what she had to say on the topic but realized she hadn't finished with a strong clause. As she thought about what she might add as a statement to emphasize she was glad to see an interruption in the form of Lucas sitting himself up straight to ask a question.

"Thank you, Stacy," he said as he began. His hands were folded together and rested on his notebook. "I'm a big fan of Toastmasters International myself so I'm always pleased to hear about the growth people experience from their involvement in Toastmasters. When you served as an officer how did you encourage greater participation? From my experience, in Toastmasters, and other all-volunteer organizations,

I've noticed it's much harder to motivate people to give their discretionary energy than it is in the workplace since many of the extrinsic motivators aren't in place."

Stacy smiled at Lucas. "Thank you for your question," she said as she unscrewed the lid from her bottled water. She wanted to buy herself a moment while she thought about the question. Although her interview prep work was open on the table in front of her, this was not a topic she'd considered and had nothing in mind. "People are motivated by a variety of things and when I try to solicit participation and support I try to appeal to something other than money as a motivator. I think of other forms of intrinsic value that inspire people. Getting to know the people I hope to serve and understanding what they care about provides me a great opportunity to add value to their lives in a variety of ways. I'm not sure if what I said answers your question or not but we were really proud of achieving 'Presidents Distinguished Club' three years in a row and I think you know that without the ability to get our team members to step up to participate in club responsibilities, it couldn't have been possible."

"I do know what it takes to run a successful club. Before I let Maria finish her question," Lucas said, generating a laugh from everyone, "Let me ask you how what you learned about motivating discretionary effort from people will apply in this role, as you understand it."

Stacy paused as she thought about her answer. "Sure, if I understand it right, Henry manages an emerging leaders program which requires

114

support from managers at all levels of the company. To have a successful program, Henry and I need to be able to get support from people we don't have any authority over. In some ways, it feels just like populating roles for a Toastmaster meeting. For example, I might succeed with some managers by appealing to their desire to help up and coming leaders but for others public recognition might be the value they seek. Finally, there might be others who will respond best to the perception that they are answering the call of duty from their superiors. It's all about understanding the people I'm trying to solicit and what their triggers are. I know that when I'm new I'll lean on Henry, and probably all of you to help make introductions and provide context. Over time, however, I'll be working to build relationships with the success of our mission in mind."

Stacy hoped that she'd answered his question well. He seemed satisfied by what she said and it didn't seem to hurt that she was able to leverage the common experience of Toastmasters. She was having a hard time reading Lucas' expression but she stopped herself from focusing on Lucas and opened her view to the full panel. "Thank you, Stacy," Maria said. "I had wanted to ask if you had any experience providing classroom instruction. I see that we're running shy on time but if you could respond very briefly that would be great."

"Yes," Stacy replied directly. "Also as a part of Toastmasters I had the opportunity to provide instruction to something called Toastmasters

Leadership Institute. It's a district-wide training session and I taught a class of about 40 people on the use of a software tracking system that can be used to keep up with the activities of each of our club's members. It was about a 40-minute training meeting."

Maria thanked her for her succinct response and asked Stacy if she had any questions for the panel.

While many of her questions had been answered either by HR, or during the interview process, the words of the sandwich evangelist came into her mind. She made eye contact with each interviewer one by one as she asked them "when you tell people you work for Powell, what is the aspect of the company that makes you most proud?"

Each of the interviewers gave responses that included comments about the sense of community, the high-quality cafeteria, certain components of the compensation package, and development programs. "I'm also very satisfied by Powell's culture," Lucas said. "I've worked at several Powell campuses and while each location's culture has strong influence from the locality, there is something consistent about what I think of as the Spirit of Powell. I believe that you will see us really living by the values declared on the posters you see around the facility. We know that what you said is true. People are motivated only so far by cash. The way to get people to put their discretionary energy into a cause is to appeal to other things they value. We believe that the alignment of values between the company and the team members is a very strong motivator, so we try to be very clear and transparent about our values so that team members can decide for themselves if they are aligned with our mission and purpose. I believe we do what we say and say what we do for our clients, for our employees, and for the environment." Lucas finally stopped speaking and someone mentioned that they'd run out of time. Stacy didn't want to let the opportunity pass to ask what the next steps would be. She learned that by Friday a decision would be made and that communications would take place early the next week. Stacy was escorted to the lobby and as she walked out into the bright sunshine, she felt good about her interview. If she could have done better, she didn't know how. She was feeling great!

Chapter 28

Stacy

Joan had been waiting all morning to hear from Stacy. She hadn't been able to focus while she thought of her friend in the interview. She was so happy to listen to every detail of the interview and took great joy in hearing about some of the answers, especially to those questions asked by Lucas. After reviewing the interview session, Joan had some additional advice she had wanted to share. Until then it hadn't been the right time. "So, you feel like you did your very best. In fact, it sounds like you think you couldn't have done any better than you did. Is that right?" Joan was asking a few questions to prepare her for the message. "You were successful in the phone screen that got you to the face-to-face and it sounds like you were successful in the face-to-face. No matter how it goes from here, you've won. Now, you only know how *you* did and what qualities and experiences you bring to the table. It's possible that there is something in another candidate's tool bag that, unfortunately you don't have. Does this make sense?" Joan paused for a moment. She hoped she hadn't come on too strong but she'd seen so many cases where the interview process led to discouragement despite a solid performance in the interview. "I want you to remember how you feel right now and let this moment give you courage, no matter how the selection process turns out."

Stacy was a little dismayed by the message because it seemed like rain during her party but she understood that Joan would only build her up and never try to harm her. They agreed that today was a day for celebration and that Stacy should spend some time looking around the town and celebrating her great performance.

She walked out to her car in the lot and stopped by a gas station for an icy cola. She drove to a nearby park and shrieked with joy as she thought about how well it had gone. She was very happy and knew she owed Joan a large debt of gratitude. Maybe she should look for a little gift while she was in town. As she thought about it she remembered her new friend at the sandwich shop. She decided to have her lunch there again today and let her know how it had gone.

Chapter 29

Henry

Henry, Paul, Maria, and Lucas agreed to debrief from the interviews over bagels in Maria's office Friday morning. "I assume you've entered the results into your spreadsheet?" Lucas said to Henry as they began the meeting. Paul was spreading cream cheese on his everything bagel and laughed softly at the teasing Lucas gave to Henry. It was a bit unlike Lucas to do it and it became clear that it was a sign of the level of respect Henry had earned lately. "As a matter of fact, I have," Henry replied, "but I guess you'd like to share your opinion of the candidates."

Maria and Paul both put their hands up as a sign of mock surrender as Henry and Lucas traded jabs in jest. Since it was Henry's position and he'd have to work most closely with the winner, all agreed that he should have the final say. As Lucas began to speak again, Henry raised his hand gently to quiet him. "I did fill out the spreadsheet but I didn't need to. We've already spoken about Larry. I think he never would have fit in here and he didn't show much ambition. I could never have chosen him. Thanks Lucas for helping me see that and for giving us the example of the kind of immediate feedback to provide right in the interview session." All three were listening to Henry speak and Maria and Paul nodded slightly at what Henry had said. Lucas had tucked his lower lip up, behind his upper teeth while he waited for Henry to share the rest of his assessment. "I had been willing to dismiss Lewis after you helped him bury himself in the interview. It was, in fact, because you defended him after the interview that I strongly considered him." Henry spoke calmly, pausing for effect. Lucas raised his eyebrows in faint surprise until Henry continued. "I strongly considered him until we met Stacy." Paul and Maria started applauding while Lucas was taking a sip of his coffee. He also showed his approval through his body language and all three smiled together over the decision. "The interesting thing is that Stacy comes from such a different background than I thought I was looking for," Henry said.

Maria tapped the tip of her index finger on the table for emphasis as she said, "That's the value of the work we did early on. The job description worksheet helped create an accurate view of what the role should and should not include. The job description was an effective way to create the advertisement for the job and identify the right competencies and skills we wanted to screen for. The Four Famous Interview Questions were applied to these tools and voila, you get the best candidate."

"Don't forget the spreadsheet," Lucas quickly threw in, in jest.

"Now, you'll have to be sure that this job description becomes a tool you'll use to set and clarify expectations and that you use it for performance management over time to ensure you are assessing her fairly and objectively," Maria said as Paul nodded in agreement. Lucas excused himself and began to leave. As he did so Henry grabbed his hand in a firm handshake and made eye contact as he expressed sincere gratitude for Lucas' time and mentoring by example. Lucas smiled in acknowledgement and made his way down the corridor.

Chapter 30

Stacy

Maria and Henry had worked with the Human resources team to organize the details of the offer for Stacy and Henry called her himself to let her know she'd been selected. Despite her excitement, she held it together while on the phone and they agreed on a start date that worked for both of them. The offer included a generous relocation package and she was excited to start her new role as part of the Powell Family. Before they hung up the phone, it occurred to her that she wasn't sure what the appropriate dress standard was for the role. Henry didn't know much about ladies' fashion but he knew enough to reply in coarse terms.

"The women here usually wear blouses and skirts or slacks. Some wear heels but many don't," as he thought about what else to say he remembered, "wearing a lot of perfume is usually frowned upon but the women usually wear small earrings and simple necklaces. I wish I could give you something a little better, I'm just not sure of the right terminology." If you'd like I can give you Maria's contact information for a better explanation. She agreed that this would be helpful and he provided the email address and phone number and they ended the call.

Immediately she called Joan and exclaimed that she'd gotten it. Joan couldn't speak right then but she expressed how happy she was to hear the news and that they should get together that night to discuss it.

By 5:30 Stacy was parked outside Joan's office as she came out at the end of the day. They hugged and squealed with joy as they revisited the news. "Do you mind driving tonight?" Stacy asked, "I think I might over celebrate a bit." She climbed into Joan's car and they started driving to a lounge they knew of.

"So, when do you start? Let me know all the details," Joan said as they drove. Stacy opened her notebook where she'd written down all the information about the offer including the dress code information. As they pulled up to the red light, Joan looked over at Stacy's note and saw something familiar about an email address written in the notebook. "Who is that?" Joan asked Stacy.

"This is the email of the lady from my interview. I think she's the HR manager at Powell and she's the manager of my new boss, Henry. He gave me her name as someone who could give me advice about the women's dress code at the site."

Joan looked at Stacy with a smile. "I know this woman. Maria was my supervisor back when I was a corporate recruiter before I came back to the university. I had no idea that she was with Powell as we haven't been in contact for years. I loved working for her. She is kind and generous with her compliments and has a strong focus on developing the strength of the people around her. In fact, it was her who got me to begin considering returning to academia after she got to know me well enough to observe my interests and skills. You know, it was when I worked with her that I learned about the Four Famous Interview Questions. It has shaped how I've done my job all these years. I'm so excited that you'll be working with her. Please feel free to convey my appreciation to her for everything she did to shape my career and perspective." Stacy could see in Joan's eyes a longing and fondness for this woman she was paying tribute to.

"I don't have to. Here's her number. You can call her yourself."

And she did.

Chapter 31

Henry and Stacy

Weeks had passed since Stacy joined Powell United. She loved her new job and had proven quickly to be a solid resource and ally for Henry. He had been able to gain all the benefits he'd hoped for with an assistant and even some that he didn't expect. Her gregarious personality opened some doors and built relationships that had been difficult to foster previously. Henry was so happy about how things had worked out. Several of the senior managers had also taken notice of the shift in trajectory of the Emerging Leaders Program which generated a stronger sense of ownership and trust in the program.

Paul approached Henry one afternoon to see how he was doing. They had spent considerably less time together since the hiring processes had been completed and he kind of missed his friend. They both had time for lunch and invited Stacy to go with them to a special event being held at the Tin Cannon Taproom. A local barbecue shop was bringing in pulled pork that had originally been earmarked for a large catering event in the community that had fallen through. Although they wouldn't drink any beer, the pulled pork sliders were only $2 until they were gone and Aaron made an excellent craft Root Beer.

"You know, Henry," Paul began as he reached for a few Jalapeño Kettle chips, "The work we did using the Four Famous Interview Questions was really great. I think we should work together to build some curriculum around that material for people who are learning how to interview candidates." Stacy dropped the sandwich she was holding in her hand as she heard him say this. At first the men didn't notice her reaction but when they did they asked what was wrong.

"My friend Joan taught me about the Four Famous Interview Questions as part of my preparation to be interviewed by you."

All three of them laughed as they finally pieced two and two together to realize that Stacy's friend Joan and Henry's boss Maria had worked together and had been the ones to formalize what both had been calling by the same name for all these years. They wondered if there were any other times when both sides of the interview table had been mentored on this same material. Again, they laughed as they thought of it.

"That settles it, then," Paul said. "We need to put together two sets of training materials on the topic. One for people learning to be interviewed," Stacy raised her hand, "and one for people who need to become good at interviewing others." Henry raised his hand.

"What would top it off is to provide a place for people to practice what they learned. Like putting together mock interviews." Stacy said this with some excitement because she knew how much she had benefitted from her mock interview experience with Joan. "The key to making the mock interviews successful is to provide a feedback loop. In Toastmasters, there is feedback on almost every activity performed in a club meeting. Every speech is evaluated as part of the meeting. The meeting roles are evaluated and some clubs even provide evaluation for the table topic speakers through feedback ballots. I guess I'm saying it's a very feedback-rich environment designed to help people improve."

Henry gave Paul a knowing look. "I know the value of feedback," he said. They rushed back to the office and agreed to work together on the project. Stacy and Henry would do the bulk of the writing and content development, but Paul could provide input and be a sounding board.

It was agreed.

Appendices

The Four Famous Interview Questions

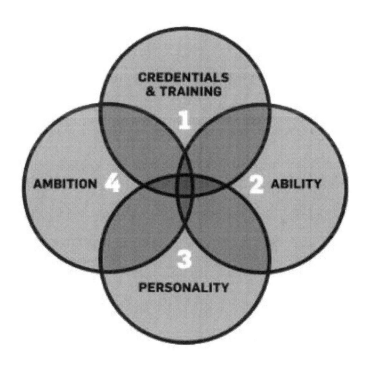

The Four Famous Interview Questions Explained

As described in the text of the Four Famous Interview Questions, the questions, in this sequence, represent four filters. If number one isn't satisfied, there's no reason to move on to number two, and so on. This doesn't mean that an interviewer will ask the questions in this sequence. They may not have even been trained to see the questions like this. The purpose of this text is to provide context to all interview questions so that candidates and interviewers alike can use them effectively and so that both can have greater success.

The Four Famous Interview Questions are as follows:

1) Does the candidate have the proper education, skills, training, certification and experience to qualify for this job?
2) Does the candidate have the ability to learn to do the job? This includes technical troubleshooting and problem solving.
3) Is the candidate's personality a good fit for the company? How well do they navigate interpersonally and how do they react to various social situations?
4) What is the candidate's ambition level? To what extent will they stretch themselves in this role and how interested are they in advancement over time?

The questions interviewers ask don't sound like these four. They're usually disguised in a different form. It's important to understand the meaning and motivation of the question and which category it belongs to. Otherwise, it may be a wasted question or distraction from what's most important. Knowing the context, or motivation for the question helps keep the conversation on track. We can skip unnecessary details that don't generate value to the questioner if we understand the meaning and motivation of the question.

This is the same table from the text.

Question	Category	How to respond
Explain how Ohms law plays into an amplification circuit.	1	
How do you verify zero energy in a gas delivery system?	1	
What is the difference between Mousse and Pudding?	1	
What are the most difficult aspects of Sarbanes-Oxley compliance?	1	
How do you recognize medication seeking behavior?	1	
What is the Roth IRA contribution limit for the current year?	1	
Explain how to make a perfect omelet.	1	Technical questions require you to relay information you've learned or problems that need solved. If you don't know the answer, talk about how you'd reason through it or determine the answer.
Explain how you have improved sales in your current role.	1	
How do you determine if a vacuum system leak is external or internal?	1	
Explain the scope of your internship/residency/etc..	1	
How do you balance the rights of the accused against public safety?	1	
How do you calculate the appropriate Furnace/AC unit for different sized homes?	1	
What is the appropriate way to set a bicycle seat for a client?	1	
What are the ingredients in a Martini/Margarita?	1	
How can you tell if you should replace or resurface rotors?	1	
Why are manhole covers round?	2	
How many golf balls would fit into a standard size train boxcar?	2	Lots of questions are geared to learning how the candidate thinks about a problem. If you don't know or if the question seems unanswerable, let the panel see how you process information and come up with a response.
How much ice would form on the leading edge of the wing of a 747 at 30000 feet?	2	
Which technology do you wish would play a bigger role in the industry?	2	
How do you know when you have put forth your best work?	3	
What do your peers say are your strengths?	3	
Do you tend to have better relationships with your superiors, peers or subordinates?	3	Questions that seek to understand how you handle a situation may be difficult so buy yourself a moment if needed to think about it. Your answer should take the approach of describing the situation, identifying the obstacles, what action you took, how it turned out and what you might do differently if you have a chance to do it again.
Provide an example of how you've dealt with a conflict in the workplace.	3	
What are our firm's values?	3	
How do you deploy a change you disagree with?	3	
How do you manage competing priorities?	3	
How have you explained to a client that what they want cannot be done?	3	Some questions are designed to understand your personality. Some don't have a right or wrong answer but are designed to understand how well you know yourself or how well you think on your feet.
When have you overstepped your role and how did you resolve the outcome of it?	3	
Describe an interaction where your boss was being unreasonable.	3	
What are you doing to strengthen your weaknesses?	3	Some questions are geared to understand how well you've prepared for the interview by researching the firm.
If you were an animal, which animal would you be?	3	
What is the best advice you've ever received and why?	3	
How have you handled disappointment in your past?	3	
How far have you gone above and beyond to provide excellent customer service?	4	The interviewer wants to know how hard you'll work to succeed in the current job and what your future plans are.
Where do you see yourself in 5 years?	4	

Preparation for Interviewers

The goal of the interviewing and selection process is to identify someone who can bring the most value to the organization and fill a specified need. Since this is true, it is important to leverage certain tools to make the process deliberate. It would be a shame to haphazardly interrogate several candidates and select one for a role for which he or she was unprepared to add maximum value.

The Job Description Worksheet is built to capture the vision of the role. In other words, if someone were to design the role from scratch to provide a certain benefit, what would the vision of that role be? Remember what Andy Stanley said about this. Identify tasks that someone else can do to enable you to do what only you can do. This requires deliberate consideration but to avoid it is to waste the remaining steps.

Once the vision of what the role will bring to the organization is created, the required talents, skills, and abilities must be identified. This is how you'll know how to satisfy your four famous questions. Here is the example Maria provided Henry. It's only a worksheet, or aid, intended to help ensure success, but remember it forms the foundation for everything else you'll do in selecting and evaluating a person in that role.

Job Description Worksheet

Powell
United

Job Title:	Department/Hiring Manager:

Purpose and vision of the role:
(What will the position add to the department?)

Key Responsibilities:
(What tasks will this person perform in order to fulfill the purpose and vision of the role?)

Key Skills and Abilities:
(What skills and abilities will this person need to perform their responsibilities?)

Required (or Preferred) Experience, Education and Certifications:
(What experiences and training are required or preferred for this role?—should be able to justify)

Exempt or non exempt employee type:	Consult with HR department for federal guidelines based on role.
Compensation level for this role:	

Using the worksheet, the information can be used to create the job description. This job description serves four purposes. Only the first of which is discussed at length in this text. The other purposes are addressed further in different books by this author.

1) It is the document from which your job posting is built.

2) It is the document you provide the employee to clarify the expectations of the job.

3) It is the document you use when conducting performance management.

4) It is the document you'd use to develop team members for this as a future role.

Here is the job description for reference from the text.

Emerging Leaders Program Assistant Coordinator

Powell United is expanding its Emerging Leaders Program to better serve the development of its employees. We are seeking someone who is enthusiastic, customer service oriented and who possesses a passion for helping others

Key Responsibilities

Essential responsibilities include (1) event planning and hosting of training sessions, (2) developing relationships with external organizations in order to solicit and arrange guest lecturers, and (3) conducting assessments of training effectiveness. Some expertise in course development and delivery is also a plus. Other responsibilities may arise, as required, from time to time.

Key Skills, Abilities and Experience

Required:

- Proficiency in MS Excel, PowerPoint, Project and Outlook
- Excellent written and spoken communication skills
- Passion for customer service
- 5 Years' experience in managing and hosting events and bookings
- Customer Service experience
- Professional appearance and demeanor

Preferred:

- Experience developing and delivering classroom instruction materials
- Experience with development and analysis of customer feedback surveys
- Experience in an employee development role

Education Required:

Bachelors of Business Administration

Once the job description is built, the specific skills are identified and the questions must be selected. One should prepare two sets of questions. One for the phone screen and one for the face-to-face interview. For the phone screen, some questions to assess education, training, and ability to learn and do the job and a question or two to begin understanding the candidate's personality are appropriate. By the time you get to the face-to-face interview, the background and training questions should be resolved leaving time for the more difficult assessment of personality fit and ambition.

Build a spreadsheet to capture candidate performance so that the decision making is objective. This helps ensure two important things: important topics won't be overlooked and all candidates will be assessed on the same criteria. Scoring the candidate real-time helps prevent panelists from letting their emotions and memories shape their decisions. Included here is the table from the text.

Candidate		Lewis Hall		Stacy Koenig		Larry Kunz	
		Raw Score	Weighted score	Raw Score	Weighted score	Raw Score	Weighted score
Criteria	Weighting						
Software skills							
Mail Merge	5	3	15	3	15	0	0
Outlook	5	3	15	3	15	3	15
Powerpoint multimedia integration	5	3	15	3	15	3	15
Excel Macro creation	5	3	15	3	15	3	15
Microsoft Project task creation	3	3	9	1	3	3	9
Event Planning							
Experience in coordinating logistics	5	3	15	3	15	3	15
Experience in guestlist management	5	3	15	3	15	3	15
Dealing with difficult people	3	3	9	3	9	3	9
Presentation experience							
Formal or informal settings (1-Toastmaster or coursework, 2-lead instruction, 3-present to managers)	3	2	6	1	3	3	9
Technical complexity of material	3	2	6	1	3	2	6
Size of audience (1-intimate <5 2-small group <15 3-large group>15)	4	2	8	3	12	2	8
Other							
Customer service	3	2	6	3	9	3	9
Management of conflicting priorities	3	2	6	3	9	2	6
Get it done mentality	4	3	12	3	12	3	12
All musts met?	yes		152	yes	150	no	143

Finally, the most important aspect of being a good interviewer is to properly use follow-up questions to challenge oversimplified or scripted answers and to help get to the true information needed to identify the best fit candidate for the role. It is a practiced and acquired skill. If there is an opportunity to interview alongside very seasoned interviewers, these sessions can provide a rich experience which can significantly aid in the development of advanced interviewer techniques. The benefit of feedback from these master interviewers, and opportunities to ask why a certain question was asked a specific way, or what motivation was at the heart of the question, cannot be overstated for its training value. Building an interviewing club with mock interviews and feedback can benefit people on both sides of the table, accelerating the ability to develop and master these skills. Be sure that questions always come from a place of authenticity and pure motive to place the best candidate and when possible incorporate guidance and feedback into the interviewing process. It may be the only opportunity to add value to that person's life and career if they are not the successful candidate.

Preparation for Candidates

Finding a position that leverages and develops your skills and abilities in a good organization with good benefits can provide great career happiness and contentment. Life satisfaction and happiness is closely tied to job satisfaction and happiness. In fact, it's very rare for someone to have happiness in their life if their job doesn't provide all these elements. Often people find that one component of their "best fit" job is missing, or they've outgrown their current role. The job search requires a person to think about what they hope to get out of their employment and should encourage them to seek positions and organizations that can satisfy their requirements. To this end, a job seeker should create his or her own statement of purpose, related to the job search. Create a list of the criteria needed to achieve that purpose and rank the list by importance. Some should be requirements that must be satisfied or the job doesn't pass muster. In some cases, the chief requirement is to provide an income and if that's where you find yourself, then satisfy the chief requirement of providing cash, and keep looking for other positions that satisfy the other requirements and preferences.

Each candidate has skills, abilities, and experience that qualify them for roles that will satisfy the criteria on their list. Certain roles require specific education, certification, and training. **Get It!** Often, opportunities to get training and education have a brief window. Do not let it pass by. Do not let certifications expire, do not fall behind on developments in your industry. In other words, always be preparing for the next opportunity, even if you are quite happy in the role you are in.

The first interview is the resume. This text is not a work on resume creation. There are many resources available in the bookstore and online. It is sufficient to say here that hiring managers need to be able to look at the resume and find the answer to the first of the Four Famous Interview Questions. Does the candidate have the required education, training, certification, or experience required to fill the role? It needs to include the degrees, certifications, skills, abilities, and experiences that job postings require. Many people find value in keeping a file that includes a collection of these attributes they can draw upon when creating custom resumes.

To prepare for a phone interview, there are three key things a person should do to prepare: research the company, understand the role, and make a list of experiences and traits that correspond to the requirements listed in the job posting. Here are the interview prep notes from the text. While not a formal worksheet, it provides an example of how to organize thoughts so they are available to draw upon during the interview.

Emerging Leaders Program Assistant Coordinator—Powell United

Helping Others

Customer Service Passion

Go extra mile for guests who want special ordered drinks. Get many repeat customers from catering jobs—elizabeth broadhurst example

Event Planning and Hosting

Governor's daughter's big wedding
State senate's new year's party

Software expertise

Microsoft Office Specialist (MOS) Master certification
Tutored students in word and excel
Created and shared excel macros to simplify bar inventory
Used vlookup and hlookup to organize catering clients for marketing
Used mail merge function to send marketing materials

Classroom Presentation

Toastmaster experience.
TLI seminar on icebreaker ideas

Education Relevance

Posting calls for bachelor although I have associates.
Classes I have completed include lower division accounting and finance, Business Strategy, Business Communication and Behavioral Theory.

Understanding and responding appropriately to the Four Famous Interview Questions is the key to performing well in the interview. Of course, bring enthusiasm and energy to any interview. Be professional and polite, selling yourself by advertising your skills and strengths.

Understand that the interviewer is trying to identify traits about each candidate that convince them which candidate is the best fit.

Remember, the interview is as much an opportunity for the candidate to assess goodness of fit as it is for the company. Prior research of the organization's mission, values, and reputation are essential to making this determination. Websites such as glassdoor.com can be useful ways to learn about a company's culture, just remember that the most satisfied employees don't tend to be the most vocal. One may learn of themes, however, that can be brought up by the candidate as questions at the close of the interview.

The selection process is comprised of many components and is not always scientific. Sometimes the best candidate is not the one who prevails and sometimes even the person who interviews strongest doesn't get selected. It can be a bit of a numbers game and there are times when not being selected for a job where the fit isn't strong is a better outcome than being selected might have been. It may be that many applications, phone and face-to-face interviews, and follow-up contacts must be made before a position is secured. Take courage from good interview performances and learn from poor showings.

In the end, the interview is just one part of the overall selection process, which happens to be filled with anxiety for the candidate, and often for the interviewer. But, so much rests on such a brief encounter for both parties that only the best performance will do. For this reason, seek out opportunities to engage in mock interview sessions. Find people who will ask you interview questions and provide you feedback on your answers. If the question is familiar and the practice of having to put experience into words is natural, the interview process doesn't need to be such an emotional event.

Good luck, you've got this!

Sample Interview Questions

The internet provides an unlimited number of interview questions customized by job category. It's an ever-growing list of questions that one can use to mentally prepare for interviews. These lists are intended for three purposes. First, use them to practice categorizing a wide variety of questions into the four famous interview questions. Second, when creating your interview prep sheet, identify experiences you have had that illustrate how well you qualify for the role. Third, find someone who will help you in mock interviews. The more practice you get answering questions, the more comfortable you will be when the pressure is on. This is just a sampling to get you started. Continue your online search to build your question library.

https://www.thebalance.com/best-interview-questions-for-employers-to-ask-applicants-1918483

https://www.monster.com/career-advice/article/100-potential-interview-questions

https://business.linkedin.com/content/dam/me/business/en-us/talent-solutions/resources/pdfs/Guide-to-screening-candidates-30-essential-behavioral-interview-questions-ebook.pdf

About the Author

Bill Ward is passionate about leadership. He has studied management styles through research and by observation and experience. This has allowed him to expand his own influence, helping people across multiple industries and volunteer organizations. Over the last twenty years, Bill has coached individuals to overcome common career mistakes. He has also taught other leaders to provide this coaching and mentoring.

Bill began working and leading in the foodservice industry. However, he has worked in the semiconductor industry for over twenty years. That is where he has supervised engineers, technicians, programmers, scientists, and other managers. He is active in his church and Toastmasters International.

The author lives in upstate New York with his wife, Lauril. They have three daughters and two sons.

To learn more about Bill's work, visit his website at www.BillWard-Leadership.com

Made in the USA
Columbia, SC
23 July 2017